Endorsements

"Leadership is a hot topic in Corporate America today—Bob Danzig nails it in *The Leader Within You*. He's found the right formula to explain and 'make real' an important yet difficult-to-explain topic."
—Richard Wagoner, Jr., President of North American Operations, General Motors

"Bob Danzig made it from office boy to corporate vice president. *The Leader Within You* helpfully reminds us that the most important stop on that journey is actually the first one—the one that begins inside each of us."
—Louis D. Boccardi, President/CEO, Associated Press

"Some books on leadership and management dwell on the obvious or the abstract. Bob Danzig's thoughtful analysis has identified the key ingredients to be mastered in leadership development."
—John J. Curley, Chairman/CEO, Gannett Co., Inc.

"Bob Danzig has been there, done that—and more. His wisdom deserves to be shared."
—David Lawrence, Jr., Publisher, *The Miami Herald*

"When it comes to leadership, Bob Danzig has lived the role. His success in our dynamic industry makes him totally qualified to speak to this quality."
—Carlo Vittorini, President, *Parade Magazine*

"As a professional colleague of Bob Danzig for more than 20 years, I've always marvelled at the magical way he seems to inspire and motivate the six thousand Hearst Newspaper employees who call him boss. It is magic, in a sense, but Bob credits his success as coming from what he calls "the leader within you," an untapped quality we all possess. Now, read and lead!"
— John Mack Carter, President, Hearst Magazine Enterprises

i

"The ability to lead does exist within everyone—Danzig has shown me and countless others how to find it, how to use it, and most importantly, how to teach others."
—Bob Schoenbacher, VP/Sales, Newhouse Newspapers

"Bob Danzig's book comes at a very good time for our industry. No one knows better than Bob the need for creative and innovative leaders, because he is one."
—Michael E. Pulitzer, Chairman, President & CEO, Pulitzer Publishing Company

"What you'll read offers the same magnetic, enthusiastic, and spirited feeling you have when visiting with Bob in person."
—Paul "Dino" Dinovitz, VP/General Manager, KMBC-TV Kansas City

"I have been in book publishing for more than thirty-five years as an author, agent and book publisher, but I have never encountered a book that is as worthwhile, stimulating and wise as *The Leader Within You*. Bob Danzig has written a remarkable book, which will be an inspiration to everyone who reads it. Bob's book can change your life." **—Bill Adler, President, Bill Adler Books, Inc.**

"The very title of Bob Danzig's *The Leader Within You* reflects the author's seasoned grasp of the essence of leadership, manifested in the gifts or 'powers' that inspire others to nourish and to develop those inner strengths."
—Bishop Howard J. Hubbard, Roman Catholic Diocese of Albany

"Able leadership comes in many shapes and styles, and it can be learned. Bob Danzig's experience will be a valuable resource for aspiring leaders."
—Frank Batten, Chairman, Landmark Communications

"Bob Danzig explains how to discover and nurture one's own leadership qualities at a new level. *The Leader Within You* is exciting, challenging and can yield dividends for those that get it right."
—Richard Harrington, President/CEO, Thomson Newspapers

"The social and technical revolutions forming the 21st century's path demand leadership from more people rather than fewer. Bob Danzig's piercing analysis and explanations will help us forge that new kind of leadership here and abroad."
—**Jean Gaddy Wilson,** *New Directions for News*

"If there ever was someone who understands—and practices—the nine powers required for leadership, it's Bob Danzig. This is a must read from a man who has lived the example."
—**Chip Weil, President/CEO, Central Newspapers, Inc.**

"Leadership can be learned. In *The Leader Within You*, Bob Danzig proves he is a premier leadership observer, practitioner and teacher." —**David Cox, President, Cowles Media Company**

"Bob Danzig knows leadership and leaders—he is one—and now he shares that expertise with all of us."
—**N. Christian Anderson, III, President and Publisher,** *The Gazette***, Colorado Springs, Colorado**

"Bob Danzig understands leadership development, especially as it relates to energy, enthusiasm, and charisma."
—**Philip Stolz, Vice President/General Manager, WBAL-TV, Baltimore, Maryland**

"A must-read for anyone who wants to become a leader in any field. Bob Danzig defines nine qualities necessary for getting to the top. In the course of his career he personified all of them."
—**Maxwell McCrohon, Former Editor:** *Chicago Tribune, United Press International, Los Angeles Herald Examiner*

"There are many perceived leaders in the world today, but a true leader is one who nurtures and masters the nine powers Bob Danzig so skillfully presents in *The Leader Within You.*"
—**David B. Carr, Senior Vice President & Chief Operating Officer, Goodson Newspaper Group**

See additional endorsements, page 153.

THE
LEADER WITHIN
YOU

THE
LEADER WITHIN
YOU

ROBERT
DANZIG
With Howard Kaplan

MASTER 9 POWERS
TO BE THE LEADER
YOU ALWAYS WANTED TO BE!

Lifetime Books, Inc.
Hollywood, Florida

Library of Congress Cataloging-in Publication Data
Danzig, Robert J., 1932-
    The leader within you / Robert J. Danzig with Howard Kaplan.
      p. cm.
    Includes bibliographical references and index.
    ISBN 0-8119-0867-4
    1. Leadership I. Kaplan, Howard, 1949- II. Title.
    HD57.7.D39 1998
    658.4 ' 092--dc21
                                  97-39570
10 9 8 7 6 5 4 3 2   CIP
Interior Design by Vicki Heil

Photo Credits:
Page 11, Lew Swyer by *Albany Times Union*; page 16, Nordstrom's by *Seattle Post-Intelligencer;* page 18,
Tiffany & Co. by AP/Wide World Photos; page 19, Phil Berman family photo; page 24, Al Neuharth by AP/
Wide World Photos; page 27, Conna Craig by Eric Millette; page 31, Rupert Murdoch by AP/Wide World
Photos; page 34, John F. Welch, Jr. by AP/Wide World Photos; page 40, Leland Stanford, Jr. supplied by
Stanford University; page 46, Nelson Rockefeller by UPI Telephoto; page 50, Ted Turner by AP/Wide
World Photos; page 56, Father Conlin by Siena College; page 62, Robert Patterson family photo; page 63,
Itzhak Perlman by AP/Wide World Photos; page 64, Max Goldstein supplied by Barbara Cohen; page 67,
Lee Iacocca by AP/Wide World Photos; page 71, Rich Ruffalo family photo; page 76, Wayne Huizenga by
AP/Wide World Photos; page 80, General John Stanford supplied by Seattle Public Schools; page 83,
Ernest L. Boyer by John W.H. Simpson; page 88, Frank Nigro by *Albany Times Union*; page 93, Aaron
Feuerstein by AP/Wide World Photos; page 96, General McDermott by *San Antonio Express News*; page
100, Gene Robb by Morris Gerber Collection; page 106, Guillermo Cristo family photo; page 112, Katharine
Graham by AP/Wide World Photos; page 115, Craig Kielburger by AP/Wide World Photos; page 119,
Beverly Sills by AP/Wide World Photos; page 126, Herb Kelleher by *San Antonio Express News*; page 130,
Billy J. "Red" McCombs by Oscar Williams; page 132, Irwin Noval family photo; page 137, David Yunich by
Albany Times Union; page 142, Frank Bennack supplied by The Hearst Corporation.

Printed in Canada

Dedication

To P.B.D.

Table Of Contents

Foreword

by Tommy Lasorda,
former manager of World Champions,
Los Angeles Dodgers

I have looked at Bob Danzig's lineup and I wouldn't change a thing. The lineup is strong from top to bottom.

I know a couple of his heavy hitters from my own field, baseball. Ted Turner didn't make his fortune from owning the Atlanta Braves, but he didn't flinch in the early years when the crowds were small and the red ink was rising. But the Braves became the team of the '90s, and Ted would have fun counting his money, if he was the kind of guy who kept count. He isn't.

Wayne Huizenga founded Blockbuster Video, so he knows what it is to win big. Still, my guess is that he found out the real meaning of the phrase, "the thrill of victory, the agony of defeat," from owning the Florida Marlins.

This brings us to a point that you will find elsewhere in these pages, but one that bears repeating. Leaders come in all types, all ages and sizes, and in different temperaments. The one quality they have in common, and without which anyone who tries to lead is doomed to fail, is confidence.

I'm lucky because I had plenty when I had nothing else. If you know who you are, and you believe in what you are doing and the company you are doing it for, other people will know it. They will follow you.

All I ever wanted in my professional life was to pitch for the Dodgers, and then to manage the Dodgers. I missed on the first goal, but it didn't stop me from succeeding on the second.

They were the Brooklyn Dodgers when I got what I knew would be my last chance to make the team, in May of 1955. The manger was Walter Alston, the man I would succeed twenty-two years later.

Alston had suspended Don Newcombe because he refused to throw batting practice. So he needs a last minute replacement to start against the St. Louis Cardinals. Who gets the start? Right. It's me. I walk a guy. A pitch gets away from my catcher, Roy Campanella. I walk another batter, Bill Virdon. Another pitch gets away. Two out, none on and I'm working on a hitter. His name is Stan Musial. A third pitch gets away. Now the runner on third comes roaring home.

Now I'm fighting for my job. There is no way he is going to score without having to cut me in half. He hits me like a truck; a pretty rugged country ball player named Wally Moon. The run scores. I strike out Musial. I strike out Rip Repulski. I get out of the inning, and in the dugout they notice my uniform is getting red around one knee.

The team has a doctor near the dugout. He examines the knee and tells me I'm through for the day. He said, "Son, if you try to pitch on that knee you may never pitch again. You've been spiked so badly, every tendon and ligament is exposed."

Not long after, the front office sent me to the minors. Before I left, I made one last appeal to Buzzie Bavasi, the general manager, and he said: "Put yourself in my chair; who would you send out?"

I told him, "There's a kid lefthander on this club who can't even throw a damned strike." Bavasi said, "Maybe, but the kid lefthander was paid a bonus to sign and the rule is that a bonus baby has to stick with the big club for two years, or else you lose him."

The name of the bonus kid who couldn't throw a strike was Sandy Koufax. Getting shipped out to the minors hurt much worse than getting spiked. But I always said, it took the greatest lefthander in history to get me off the Dodgers.

There are executives who tell their stories, in this book, that will cover the full range of what it takes to be a leader. My list might be a little different from anyone else's, but mine would include pride, loyalty, a sense of humor and persistence.

I once asked Pee Wee Reese where he would have rated me, among the 25 Dodger ball players in 1955, as a prospect to manage a big league club. Pee Wee said 24th, and that was because one guy, Sandy Amoros, didn't speak English.

I proved a lot of people wrong and I did so for twenty years. We went to the World Series four times and won it twice. I was lucky to have the players I had, and luckier to have the only job I ever wanted. Between myself and Walter Alston, the Dodgers had only two managers in forty-five years. This was an incredible run, when you consider that neither of us ever had a contract longer than one season. The O'Malleys, Walter and his son, Peter, didn't give long-term contracts — and they didn't fire people on a whim.

There is a pretty good leadership lesson right there.

❒   ❒   ❒

Preface: The Formed Leader

I t has been my observation that, although leadership qualities may be inherent, the so-called "born-leaders" are really those who spent their lives as works in progress. It is the *"formed-leader"* who lights the way through example.

The oak tree is formed from the acorn; we're formed via the effects our home, education, work, peers, relatives, friends and environment have on us. All are stepping stones to help us cross the water ways of life. We may be born with leadership powers, but without the proper development, their potential may be blunted. You can wait to be formed or you can take an active role in your own creation by being open and receptive to those around you, who share the qualities of their leadership. Take a moment to think about people who have influenced you and why you think this is so. Why do you remember certain people or mentors from your early years?

Throughout school, college and graduate work, we are about learning, about obtaining the credentials necessary to become part of the American workplace. Once there, the next step is to learn skills that will prepare us to be managers. These learning steps are largely reflective of what people have done all their lives, since kindergarten; they have learned skills, aptitudes and information to move them to the next plateau.

The wonder of your inherent leadership characteristics is that they do not need to be learned. They are innate; they only need to be formed, nurtured and cultivated.

All of us have the leadership powers, which allow us to lead our lives in a more effective and satisfying way, within us. Once identified and activated, these freshly-honed characteristics within our individual acorn can result in our becoming leaders, and will dramatically change the kind of people we are.

In our historic culture of progress and growth, I believe, the core lubricant for growing your personal oak tree is nourishment of the leader within you. Through my experiences, I've come to view leadership as a series of powers that do not have to be learned, because the potential for leadership is within every single person, regardless of age, background or position. Whether you're focused on living your own life with greater serenity, on your way to middle-management, or beaming your eyes on the prize of leading others effectively — you can better achieve your ultimate goals by nurturing the leader within you.

My career in the newspaper business — and with Hearst — began nearly fifty years ago when I was office boy at the *Albany Times Union,* in upstate New York. Nineteen years after I walked in the door, in 1969, I was named publisher of that newspaper, and shortly after, became the youngest person to lead the New York State Publishers' Association. As senior executive guiding all Hearst newspapers for the past two decades, I've been privileged to be at the helm of one of the top ten newspaper companies in the nation. In that time, we've experienced a renaissance of talent, technology, and reputation. During this expansion, newspaper acquisition investments have exceeded more than three-quarters of a billion dollars. I believe that our newspapers are positioned as they are today — perched for further success in the new millennium — because we have encouraged the development of the leadership qualities and characteristics inherent in so many of my colleagues.

My positions and experiences have given me the unique opportunity to have personal contacts with some of the most influential leaders of our time. The media that I have immersed myself in for nearly half a century has given me access to leaders at the top of their chosen fields. My personal experiences have enabled me to observe leaders, who, in turn, have provided me insights to a unique power of leadership reflected within them.

From the smallest business to the world's institutional giants, all depend on leaders for guidance and direction; everyone has the natural equipment to lead, to impact their personal future and, perhaps, the destiny of others.

In the past few years, I've taken my leadership message on the road and have addressed enthusiastic audiences in corporate and university settings. Whether I'm addressing a group at Harvard University, an audience of managers in the mid-West, or a business class at the New School, people are intensely curious about their own leadership capabilities and potentials. Whether it's Cambridge or Kansas, this is a topic that resonates in the hearts and minds of people of all ages.

The wide range of people I meet are uniformly grateful for the opportunity to have someone address their own unique leadership potentials. Most people are hungry to bring positive change into their lives. My message of leadership possibility is simple and accessible to all who are open to receive it.

For example, many have never really thought of what the characteristic of **quality** means to them, but a short time after we discuss it, they want to develop that personal attribute, not only for themselves, but for friends, family, and colleagues. They recognize that this powerful characteristic, once actively shared, will make others aware of their own leader impulses within.

I've tapped into a genuine appetite in the marketplace for personal change and the recognition that all people have the potential to be leaders, if only in the attitudes about how they lead their own lives.

The Leader Within You has a straightforward objective: to encourage people to be active participants in shaping their own future through self-knowledge, and reflections about how we've all been indelibly touched by people who have crossed our paths. These threads of life, accidental or not, bring us into contact with people who have the ability to enhance our lives and to help us weave a more brilliant tapestry of our own life stories, in subtle or ever-lasting ways.

My belief is simple: By spotlighting the leaders who have crossed my path, you, the reader, will be able to identify your most important leader — **the leader within.**

—Robert J. Danzig

Acknowledgment

F or the lifelong "you can do it" inspiration of Patricia Brady; the ever-flowering Mary Beth, Marsha, Darcy, Steven, Matthew, Charles and Miles; the patient competence of Marge Murphy, Yvette Harris, Christine Gray; the embroidery of poet-collaborator, Howard Kaplan; the well-grounded eye of editor Hillel Black; the affirmation of value of Donald Lessne; the sharp editing of Callie Rucker and all those Hearst Newspaper colleagues whose threads of life helped weave my personal tapestry.

Introduction

The Science of Management,
The Art Of Leadership

For the past half decade, many of us have had the feeling of leaving the table a little bit hungry; the "management meal" we've been served has not quite hit the spot with its limited menu of retrenchment and competitive down-sizing. It is so palpable that people at large are hungering to see the ingredients of leadership join us at the table. Every single person can be encouraged to trigger a new awareness that encourages those leadership qualities to shine. That fresh insight can benefit each individual and have rippling effects for those who are in positions of promise.

Over the last five years or so, many thoughtful observers believe our nation has endured a period of extraordinary emphasis on the science of management, resulting from the very real concerns that accompany a changing society. As we've moved toward the millennium, we've experienced changing global requirements for more competitive businesses and institutions, which have often resulted in employee downsizing and restructuring. This has been true not just for businesses, but for hospitals, institutions of education and the arts as well. Everyone has had to respond to a changing economic environment and the main response has been weighted toward the science of management — measuring, allocating and directing our human resources.

With all this focus on the smaller management picture, the larger leadership picture — and what institution is not itself comprised of big and little pictures — has lost its focus. If the inordinate emphasis of an organization is on the management of resources, the downsizing of employment, the farewell to businesses that can no longer contribute as they have in the past — if that's all that is done, then the spirit and soul of that enterprise is going to be diminished.

Management is an essential fundamental requirement of the operation of all civil societies, including business, health care, arts and educational institutions. We cannot deliver 10 million Hearst newspapers to readers each week without a carefully calibrated and managed process. Management is of the utmost importance. However, when separating the two like strands of a rope wound tightly together, the discreet elements suggest that management is about today and leadership is about tomorrow. Management is a series of learned attributes; leadership relies on inherent capabilities. Management is about process; leadership illuminates vision and promise.

Put another way, all leaders are also managers of others. But not all managers exercise the qualities of leadership.

If this sounds a bit too simple, examine for a moment that rope of leadership. Or think of it like those strands of DNA that are found in your genes. When you were born you had within you the capacity for all of the common powers of leadership in this book. They do not have to be learned because they belong to your being even though they may lie dormant forever until you exercise them.

Dance pioneer Martha Graham used to say, "Everyone is born with genius, but most people lose it after fifteen minutes." Allow me to replace the word genius with leadership. Both words to me are synonymous with people who know themselves and choose to release all their shining qualities within. Perhaps that's what really makes a genius — the ability to know oneself so well you send out an inspirational beam just like a lighthouse.

❏   ❏   ❏

Let me outline a few reflections on the results of reliance so weighted on the scale to the science of management:

☐ A nation of employment drifters with no long term sense of institutional loyalty is not a nation that cultivates progress.

☐ An atmosphere of fear of impending joblessness is not an atmosphere that motivates risk.

☐ The priorities that inspire momentum must include more than becoming the smallest possible entity of human endeavor.

Progress. Risk. Momentum. Where would you or we be without them?

Many in the American workforce have been traumatized, victims of the excessive reliance on the science of management. It is timely to address the issue of how the nation's free enterprise structure is answering the questions — *Now what? What's next?*

I see the cultivation of the art of leadership as the balancing answer on the scale to ignite loyalty to purpose, creative risk-taking and momentum with velocity.

Indeed, while management preserves, and can build some short term economic progress, it is leadership that infuses the dreams, inspires the visions, and causes people to respond with vigor for the long haul. The science of management cannot be expected to unleash human potential. Your personal life can be <u>managed</u> efficiently, yet lack the rich satisfaction of being <u>lead</u> well. It is leadership that paints a broader vision and inspires people to join in the acquisition and fulfillment of that vision, by lubricating each individual's creative capabilities.

I perceive the maintenance of organizations and the required functioning on a day-to-day basis to be achieved by management; it is the essential glue to the calibrated process every business requires. Leadership, however, is what builds greatness in people and institutions.

☐ ☐ ☐

The following queries are offered to help navigate the crossing from sterile management to true leadership.

☐ What are the tools to cross the bridge from the management which aims to achieve an organization's leanness and so-called competitive fighting weight, to the spirited leadership, that builds institutional greatness?

☐ Can you stimulate your colleagues to climb the higher mountains of success now that you and they know how to measure the mountains and allocate the precise resources of human and equipment needs for the tasks at hand?

☐ Can you motivate a well-managed but perhaps cynical staff to believe in and participate in "growing" your future together?

☐ Is the art of leadership nourishing the spirit and soul of your workplace?

In the final analysis, only a motivated people can participate in expanding the innovation highway that stretches the boundaries of the possible for the people, businesses and institutions which will shine in the future. That motivation is vested in the leader. It is not found in bricks or budgets. It resides in the vision of the leaders who are the architects of tomorrow — they master the following nine leadership powers that are within them and within you:

QUALITY

INNOVATION

INSPIRATION

PERSEVERANCE

PASSION

CHARACTER

CHARISMA

ENERGY

ENTHUSIASM

A Mind's Eye Picture

This is the anatomy of leadership I have observed. Sometimes I think it resembles the clear pages in an old Gray's Anatomy textbook — one of those cellophane inserts where the complete picture of a man (or woman) is formed only after the proper number of pages have been turned, one on top of the other. The first page might give you only the outline of a man, but after turning half a dozen or so pages, all the vital parts — blood, tissue, the works — of a human being are filled in. Anything less than the whole picture is worthless.

The nine powers listed are essential to the spirit that can renew and re-ignite the inventiveness, determination, fidelity and sense of opportunity which inspire workers of the nation. What's more, these nine powers of leadership are inherent in everyone; the promise to live a life of greater satisfaction pulses in you and every individual. You have the ability to nourish those inherent leadership abilities as you progress through each stage of your life. That is a two-fold gift: by awakening the leader within, you can inspire the leader without. See if by focusing on your own leadership characteristics, you don't find yourself leading your own life more successfully. That promise is profound.

Although everyone can identify other characteristics they admire in leaders, the odds are high that those individuals also have the common powers identified here. The good news for all who have the opportunity to build a life ripe with success for today and tomorrow is that these are inherent gifts that everyone can cultivate and use.

But what about those qualities that cannot be so readily identified, for example, soul. It breathes in the lungs of leaders and flows in their blood. It won't show up in an x-ray and a blood test won't indicate the level of soul that's circulating in the body. You can't go to the gym to firm up your soul by climbing a soul-master. What exactly is soul and how does it relate to leadership, business and work?

Spirit, belonging, individual identity, a sense of worthiness, control and competency are self-esteem essentials in the view of noted author Dennis Weatley; the soul of any individual, as well as any organization is manifest in the collective self-esteem of that entity. Morale, cohesion, achievement, and quantum leaps of breakthrough thinking, are all reflections of the soul of the enterprise. At the end of the day, it is the leader who cultivates and nourishes his own and the collective organizational spirit. Managers can speak to the body of the structure. It is the leader who nurtures its soul.

In the pages that follow, we will "walk the walk" with successful people who have crossed our path — each of whom has exhibited **Quality, Innovation, Inspiration, Perseverance, Passion, Character, Charisma, Energy** and **Enthusiasm**. Some have been subtle threads in the tapestry of my life, others more complete patterns of brilliant mosaics which have come my way. Some are less known. Others are towering confirmations of public success. All are typical of many people the reader has known.

❏   ❏   ❏

PART ONE

The Tapestry of Life

☐ Management Fuels The Body

☐ Leadership Fires The Soul

☐ Your Threads Of Life

Sometimes people only cross your path for brief moments, but in that time, they give you a glimpse of their gift to lead. Although the thread they weave may seem short and insignificant in relation to you, it could turn out to be the integral strand needed to make the tapestry of your life shine.

The other day, while rolling up a handmade Indian rug, I took notice of the underside which nobody sees. You could see the effort and imagine the work that went into the series of knots and threads sewn together. There was a pattern on the underside of the rug, but it wasn't as beautiful as the top side everyone saw; its rough back face was only on show for the floor.

When I think about the threads of life, of what people have given me and of what I'm able to give to others, I think how similar this is to that hand-made rug. The tapestry of life is formed by individual threads, taken together to form a whole. You may not see the knots and the rough spots, you may not see the work and the effort, but they're all in place, allowing you to walk on a smoother path. Be aware of those who can provide you with the vital threads of life needed to make your tapestry a breathtaking work-in-progress.

❏ ❏ ❏

PATHMAKERS AND KINDLERS

A kindler nation best occurs when it is populated by kindlers, those who inspire others to help build the institutions that will shape the future.

All my life I have received inspiration from people who have crossed my path. Many times, I did not necessarily know what exactly it was about them that profoundly influenced me, but upon reflection, it was a thread of life in them, a characteristic of leadership that caused me to be conscious of them. In turn, that enabled me to become conscious of my own leadership possibilities; these are the kind of people who not only burn with an internal light, they also act as kindlers, by enabling that flame to be passed on and brighten another person's life.

How did I first become aware of kindlers and pathmakers? An open heart, an open mind and an open path led me to them. I did not grow up in a traditional family; I was raised in five foster homes. My mother and father divorced when I was two. Afterwards, I lived for a short period of time with my mother who was seriously ill. I believe I became open to influence by people whose threads of life offered goodness, because such a quality was vacant from my ordinary circumstances. My early years were spent surviving, getting through and learning how to adjust to new, constantly changing, alien circumstances.

School was something I simply had to endure each day; I learned enough to pass each year, but many basic lessons just didn't take. What I mainly learned about during those early foster home years was survival. More importantly, I learned to be open to the examples offered by good people. I don't know why that is. Perhaps if I was totally aware at the time, this wouldn't have happened; I just locked into a quality in these people that stayed with me. This is how I know that those I met along the way did more than just cross my path.

There was something in my welcoming attitude that attracted those people into giving me more of themselves than a perfunctory relationship would have done. These people caught my attention not because they were effective managers, but because they impressed me with some larger characteristic that emanated from them; that keenly developed characteristic found a way to become a part of the weave making up my life tapestry. I believe leadership powers are elements in the souls of those people.

As I moved from office boy to clerk, junior salesman to retail advertising manager, business manager to general manager, and finally publisher of the newspaper to two decades as head of the whole newspaper company nationwide, I tried to develop the fundamental powers in myself that were inherent in the people who crossed my path.

◻ ◻ ◻

IT ALL STARTED WITH A HAT

At a dance on the evening of October 16, 1950, I ran into one of my high school buddies. He told me that his office boy position in the circulation department at the *Albany Times Union* was available because he was being promoted to clerk. After saying he thought it would be a good idea for me to apply for the job, he added some sage advice, "You know, you're only seventeen, and look a bit younger than that. Why don't you get yourself a hat? That should do the trick."

I took his words to heart; that night I went to the Snappy Men's Shop on Albany's Central Avenue, and bought the first hat I ever owned. The next morning, I waited in line behind eight other applicants, feeling properly dressed for the job, at least from the neck up. The hat topped off the look like an exclamation point on a sentence; I was ready.

The line moved slowly, as one by one, we were admitted into the office. When my turn came, I was met by Margaret Mahoney, a no-nonsense lady who gave me and my not-too-impressive resume, the once over; I had no prior work experience and had just finished high school. Instead of asking me questions related to the job, she looked at me and said, "I'd like to ask you one question."

"Yes, Ma'am."

"Why are you wearing that hat?"

I explained how my friend had recommended it, and she gave me one of those "oh, really" looks, when I told her, "I never had a hat before, and didn't know what to do with it, so I left it on."

"Yes," she said, between a grimace and a smirk, "but people take their hats off when they come inside the building, and you've had yours on now for about an hour and a half." Then she offered me the job.

I believe I was hired because Margaret Mahoney couldn't get over the fact that I didn't know enough to take my hat off. That incident seemed to create a bond between us, and, more importantly, gave me a pathmaker at the *Times Union*.

Though Margaret Mahoney was the office manager, she considered herself the unofficial Ambassador of the *Albany Times Union*. She took me under her wing and advised me, "When somebody calls in to place an order or to make a complaint, I am the ambassador; I am the last contact from the paper for that person. If I treat that customer as royalty, then that customer will have a positive view of this newspaper." She infused that notion of customer royalty on an every day basis.

In 1993, I went to the employee quarter-century club celebration in Albany. Across the room I spotted Margaret Mahoney, now long retired. I gave her just as much respect that night, as I did when I handed her my application for office boy. That night, however, I took my hat off to her for being the pathmaker who taught me the lessons of customer royalty and loyalty.

◻ ◻ ◻

Another early kindler was a salesman at the *Albany Times Union* named Manny Kripps. He was a very distinguished and energetic person who overwhelmed his customers with service. At the time, I was a teenage classified advertising salesman and Manny was an experienced senior classified salesman who harbored an extraordinary dedication to excellence. He dressed with excellence, carried himself with excellence and treated his customers with excellence. He took me under his wing while I was getting used to classified advertising. One morning a week I'd go out with him. He always told me, "Your job is to watch the way we deal with our people; watch why it is important to give complete service to each customer."

Manny spent his entire life as a classified advertising salesman. He tackled this relatively modest work every day and always chose to excel because *that* characteristic was inherent in his person. "No matter what you do, be the best," he'd say. He struck a chord in me and showed me how to tune into excellence.

Nineteen years after landing the job as office boy and going to college nights, I was named publisher and met Agatha O'Neil. She had been the personal assistant to the two publishers before me for a total of twenty years. On my first day as publisher, she greeted me, sat me down and said, "Let me tell you how things are."

I said the same thing to her that I said to Margaret Mahoney so many years before, "Yes, Ma'am."

"The paper has been losing money for thirteen consecutive weeks, and it looks like we're about to hit fourteen, she began. All ten of our labor contracts have expired, the unions are threatening to strike, and we are forty-five days behind schedule on building a new newspaper plant; that's where you are."

"Miss O'Neil," I said, "I'm afraid it gets a little worse than that. In all my years at the newspaper, I've never spent a single day in the accounting department." I told her that I had never seen a profit and loss statement or a balance sheet, and had no idea what they meant.

"Well, I've seen them for twenty years," she said, brushing aside any fears that this was going to be an obstacle.

Two days later, she sat me down next to her at the conference room table. The first thing she did was point to the bottom of page one of the profit and loss statements, and ask, "Do you see those brackets?"

"Yes, Ma'am," I answered.

"Those brackets are not good news. Your job is to get rid of the brackets."

Every week, during my first year as publisher, Agatha O'Neil tutored me on the details surrounding P & L statements. She gave me a grounding by showing me the essence of our business and gave me insight, just as Margaret Mahoney had given me insight about customer royalty; she was a kindler to me.

When we eliminated the brackets, I attributed our success, in large measure, to the infusion of customer royalty and quality service into the spirit of the paper. We were able to increase circulation, solve the labor issues, and move into our smashing new headquarters on the site of a former pumpkin patch.

More importantly, we were able to amplify the quiet pitch of quality commitment to every customer into an appreciable roar.

Ask yourself now: Who have been your kindlers and pathmakers?

Do you know yourself well enough to let others be kindled by you?

□ □ □

❝ There is no greater customer in your life than the one sitting in your chair. You are the most important customer you will ever have and you should treat yourself with customer royalty. When brackets enter your life, use the nine powers of leadership within you to delete them. Be open to the pathmaker kindlers in your life, and lead your life with the commitment to be a pathmaker and kindler for others.

Two kindler ladies and an inspired salesman taught me that management without spirit and soul is incomplete. Leadership makes a place complete. ❞

FOCUS AND PURPOSE: MEETING THE LEADERS

The trappist monk Thomas Merton is the author of "Seeds of Contemplation," a beautiful book of ideas. As I developed the thoughts about *The Leader Within You*, my mind repeatedly returned to the basic lesson of Thomas Merton: there is a wondrous value in pausing to contemplate that which has crossed our path.

I have included such invitations for your reflections in a series of "Interludes" in this book. They offer a small oasis for your contemplation, as you read the brief descriptions of the lives of the leaders who have crossed my path.

The *Leader Within You* now turns to figures who have mastered the nine powers of leadership you are ready to develop. *Quality* is a good place to start and acts as a strong foundation for the life improvement prospects we will explore together.

❑   ❑   ❑

PART TWO

The Power Of Quality

☐ Propensity To Excel

☐ Seek Standard Above Norm

☐ Leader in Conduct, Aspirations, Relationships

Imagine that you've arrived at your desk in the morning. After settling in, turning on your computer and waiting for the menu, you notice something new on the screen — the letter "*Q*". You click on it twice, and the word *quality* appears. You click on it again and "congratulations, you've just chosen to begin your day with a commitment to quality, and to proceed in all your undertakings, both professional and personal, in the same manner," appears on the screen. What is quality? *It is the propensity to excel — to seek a standard above the norm which is inherent in every person.* Leaders rely on this characteristic to be a beacon of light in their conduct, aspirations, and relationships. Leaders do not take detours which divert quality. Leaders seek out a higher ground and set the pace for others to embrace.

How far are you from quality? The answer is not very far. You have the capacity for quality within you. You recognize quality in those heightened elements that are part of your everyday life and are comforted by them. Envision your own inherent gift of quality.

You may not have noticed the "**Q**" on your computer's menu before, but once you've chosen it, there's no turning back.

Quality initiates your awareness of everything else on your menu. You take your mouse and click again on the word **quality**, and what comes up? **Innovation.** It is an interesting word choice, considering you're convinced that the idea you've been tossing around in the back of your head will help to improve the quality of not only your life and your work, but that of those around you.

So **quality** has taken you to **innovation**, and clicking again on **innovation** reveals **inspiration**. Ah ha, you think as a lightbulb turns on in your head. You're totally inspired. One of the plusses of inspiration is that it gives off a light, allowing others to follow your lead, if they wish. Now you're on a roll. You click again to reveal the final sequence of words: **perseverance, passion, character, charisma, energy and enthusiasm.**

Relax for a second while you read the words on the screen one more time. Try and think of a person who you believe is an outstanding example of one or more of these characteristics; it shouldn't be that difficult. Perhaps even your name is floating among the possibilities.

QUALITY

❝ Leaders choose quality. They set their own standards of quality performance high and inspire those around them to do the same. ❞

LEW SWYER

A lot of who I am can be attributed to pivotal experiences occurring during my years in Albany, New York as a young publisher. This includes meeting and working with Lew Swyer, who became Chairman of the Board of the Saratoga Performing Arts Center, summer home to both the New York City Ballet and the Philadelphia Orchestra.

Those of us who served on the Performing Arts Center Board of Directors with Lew were inspired first hand by his attention to quality and dedication to achieve beyond the norm. He insisted that every event be on time, and advocated the notion of having the trash barrels on the grounds emptied, when half full, so patrons always had the sense of a manicured environment.

Lew Swyer

Lew often scheduled the Board of Directors meeting behind the stage at rehearsals of the Philadelphia Orchestra and New York City Ballet. He urged every board member to be personally immersed in the world-class quality of both and stressed that the premier talent on the board had to have their commitment to excellence reflected in the finished product of everything they did; they had to have the Midas touch.

Quality was his constant goal. When the Philadelphia maestro raises his baton, and when the dancers from the New York City Ballet take to the stage, excellence permeates every aspect of their performance. Lew's leadership nurtured the magnificence that makes every Saratoga summer evening magic.

Only quality was woven through Lew's life. Similarly, Lew only offered such excellence as his addition to the tapestries of others.

Although he studied drama and not business, at Johns Hopkins University, Lew became one of the largest and most distinguished commercial builders of office buildings, shopping centers and other retail operations in the Albany area.

Since we served on many of the same boards, we became fast friends. Every Saturday morning, Lew would come to my office at the *Albany Times Union,* where, over a pot of coffee, we would philosophize and think of ways to improve the quality of life in the Albany area; we were true friends who relished the same activities and each other's company.

Lew and I also served together on the board of St. Peter's Hospital. I watched how Lew, as Chairman of the Board of Directors, became an advocate for integrating spirituality into patients' healing programs. His advocacy resulted in a new spiritual care office to be manned by professionals and volunteers. Lew personally wrote out the quality standards of spiritual care each patient deserved and requested that the Board of Trustees participate in the quality care training that each member of the new spiritual care office would have. His dedication to a full spiritual care program infused itself into every aspect of the hospital. Lew established a regular patient monitor research discipline that evaluated the quality of care each patient experienced — physical and spiritual.

His leadership mantra for every board member, administrator and medical professional, was that the flag we must all salute was the flag of quality care. Every hospital patient benefited from his personal standard of quality; he breathed it into the entire institution.

Unfairly, Lew, a majestic man of almost six and a half feet, developed cancer; his body deteriorated as the cancer invaded his spine. It was with great difficulty that he shuffled along with his cane during one of my Saturday morning visits.

Our last meeting was bittersweet. We had shared the same goals and had been both friends and colleagues for such a long time; it seemed impossible that we would part this way. I told him he needed to know that I would always relish the rich and everlasting quality of his friendship and ability to lead.

When I returned home that evening, the phone rang as I walked in the door. I picked it up; it was Lew. Unbeknownst to me, the answering machine recorded our conversation. My daughter, Darcy, saved the tape. "Bob," he began, "While I have some breath and stamina, I want to tell you how much your visit meant to me today. I also want you to know that our Saturday morning visits are a rich reservoir for me. We may have tilted at some windmills, but our lances were poised, and I do believe we achieved some good things." I still have that tape.

There is a life size bronze statue of Lew in a downtown park. When I return to Albany, I often visit that statue, reflect on the great quality of Lew Swyer's leadership and quietly whisper, "Through your leadership emphasis on quality, you achieved many lasting things; some of us were privileged to walk that walk with you."

REFLECTIONS ON
L E W I S   A .   S W Y E R

Characteristic of QUALITY
By: Annette Covatta, SNJM
Sister of the Holy Names

*T*hat Lew Swyer be distinguished for the characteristic of quality in leadership does not surprise me. From our first meeting in 1968, Lew exemplified quality as a beacon in everything he pursued, in every human encounter and, yes, in every breath he took. It was an inherent gift. A hallmark of his unique persona.

In 1967, I dreamed of building an arts center in Albany, NY, where children and adults could discover their creative processes by learning and experimenting with multiple art forms. I received encouragement from a number of civic leaders I knew in the community. Without exception, as each interview ended, I heard the same question, "By the way, have you talked to Lew Swyer?"

About one year later, Lew met with me on a Sunday morning. As I shared my vision, I was struck by the quality of his listening. He was totally present to every nuance. He asked questions in order to understand and grasp all the dimensions of the project, not unlike the visitor at an art gallery who takes in the whole canvas, the macro view, before focusing on the details. His questions revealed a quality of probity that stretched my thinking far beyond the parameters of my vision. Now that is leadership permeated by quality! What astounded me further was that I did not get to ask for his help. He offered!

Every meeting became an experience of expansion and creation, always grounded in reality, always enthusiastic and engaged, always challenging and cajoling me to dream big, take risks, think through, focus, and, above all, pay attention to the inner stirrings shaping the vision and fine tuning its form. In other words, to be a discerning, not a foolish, creator!

On one occasion, as we sat in the parlor of his home, the conversation veered to the subject of spirituality: the invisible world, the inner life, beliefs and God. At one point, Lew said, "I believe in the God of Excellence and Achievement." The statement came forth with a conviction that welled up from the core of his soul. I knew then the secret of his indomitable energy.

Lew's high standards of quality energized and inspired me to reach for the fullness of my potential. The fire of quality that burned in everything he touched, ignited in me such bold decisions as applying for admission in Harvard University's prestigious Institute in Arts Administration and in the groundbreaking Creative Problem-Solving Institute of the University of Buffalo. I wonder if I would have aimed that high were Lew not there, nudging and encouraging me not to settle for less.

It is often said that the quality of our dying is the consequence of the quality of our living. In other words, we die as we live. Lew lived two years longer than was expected by his doctors. Not surprising. His ubiquitous presence, helping others, encouraging talented performing and visual artists through sponsorship and attendance, actively advancing or changing agendas of the multitude of boards and committees he was part of, and committing fully to every cause he believed to be worthwhile, all contributed to transforming the physical and humanitarian landscape of the Capital District.

In his dying, the quality of his presence and leadership continued to be active. When he was too weak to be physically

*present, he communicated by phone or in writing. Lew died in
the last hour of Christmas Day 1988. In his hospital room were a
few bags of Christmas gifts yet to be delivered.*

*I shall never forget one Saturday afternoon on a beautiful
Autumn Day when Lew dropped by my office, bringing me a
45" disc. It was a recording of Desiderata, an anonymous poem
of sheer illumination. Threads of the text poured over me like
music:*

"Go placidly amid the noise and the haste . . .

"Speak your truth quietly and clearly . . .

*"Whatever your labors and your aspirations, keep peace
with your soul..." Listening to the words, I glanced over at him.
This man, towering over 6 feet in height, seemed like a little
boy, discovering, as if for the first time, the unmitigated mystery
of life in its essence and purest quality.*

POSSIBILITIES

NORDSTROM'S & TIFFANY'S

Whether your name is Manny Kripps, or Louis Comfort Tiffany, one of your over-riding objectives is complete customer service and satisfaction. You could be Margaret Mahoney urging employees to treat customers like royalty in Albany, or John Nordstrom in Seattle, at the turn of the century. Each jewel shines best in the proper setting.

For this reason, though this is a book about the leader within, I've chosen to highlight two institutions (it's hard to call them stores) that have taken customer service beyond the once-imaginable. Each is an example of how the inner power of quality can be made manifest in the outside world. Remember, in each case, it all started with one person's dream and vision . . .

You never know if your idea is going to catch on. You never know if your little store on New York's lower East side will one day move to prestigious Fifth Avenue, with shops that glow on expensive boulevards in the major capitals of the world.

❏   ❏   ❏

NORDSTROM'S

Once you've shopped there, it's hard to go any place else. Nordstrom's is committed to giving customers quality service from the time they enter the store, to the time they leave, purchases in hand. Recently, my son Matt and I visited the local Nordstrom shoe department, where we felt we would find a full selection of shoes for his size twelve feet. After the salesperson cheerfully trotted out numerous shoes, we bought one pair, and placed an order at another branch for a second pair. The salesman completed the transaction, signed his name and "thanks" on the sales slip, and came around the counter to shake Matt's hand and tell him how grateful he was for the business.

On the way home, we stopped at a different large department store to browse through their shoe department. We asked the young sales person on duty whether he had a size 12 in the style my son had chosen. Without comment, he went into the inventory room, returned with one shoe box, laid it on the floor, and tossed a shoe horn on the floor next to the shoes. He stood to the side to watch Matt try on the shoes by himself, and clearly had no interest in whether the shoes were sold. They were not.

Nordstrom's

16

The contrast of the two back-to-back experiences magnified the different commitments to quality service. The Nordstrom principle of providing service beyond the norm started with one person. That person decided to commit to quality and provided the leadership to perpetuate that commitment.

John Nordstrom left his native Sweden, at the age of sixteen, and arrived in New York with five dollars in his pocket. Unable to speak a word of English, he proceeded to work his way across the country to Seattle.

In 1901, partners Wallin and Nordstrom opened their first small Seattle shoe store. When the store first opened, the young partners bought shoes in all medium size ranges, only to discover that the sizes were not large enough for their big boned Swedish friends. Immediately, they began carrying larger and wider sizes. This launched their reputation for having a wide variety of inventory in stock. This reputation aged well and continues to be a cornerstone of Nordstrom's today.

The fundamental foundation of Nordstrom's is not about inventory, it is about quality service and the careful training of each Nordstrom employee, since 1901, to be a link in the solid chain of John Nordstrom's commitment to quality. His commitment was so profound that it has permeated the generations of management which followed him.

Organizational cultures do not arrive out of nowhere. They are the products of a person who brings the energy of leadership to that culture. In this case, walking in the footsteps of John Nordstrom is a very satisfying experience.

□ □ □

TIFFANY'S

Success is to be celebrated. I have often saluted the achievements of my colleagues throughout the nation by a recognition gift to their spouses. Flowers often flow from my office to the wives of achievers; they are always a welcome way to spotlight the triumph of a loved one. However, the most beautiful notes of thanks are prompted by the delivery of an item from the premier jeweler Tiffany's. When the Tiffany box arrives to celebrate achievement, that spouse knows the celebration is very special.

Flowers and Tiffany's have been a signature tradition for recognizing my associates. The flowers take their beauty from nature; the Tiffany's gift takes its beauty from the nature of a man who put quality first.

Tiffany & Co.

The year was 1830. The location was Broadway in lower Manhattan. Tiffany was one of many small jewelry stores. Owner Charles Lewis Tiffany had a singular commitment to quality that distinguished his store above all the others. His leadership skills developed the store and made it grow to become a great institution, sought out by shoppers throughout the world.

Charles polished quality in every aspect of his store. Personnel were selected because they went beyond accepted behavior. Fixtures, store furnishings and repair service all emphasized quality. Even today, over a century and a half later, anyone receiving that blue box instantly knows it contains an item of the highest quality; it is a reflection of the majestic name, Tiffany's, a perpetual legend born of the founder's leadership commitment to quality.

Like Charles Lewis Tiffany, we can all commit ourselves to quality. What's more, you really don't need to learn the concept. It is always a part of you. You need only choose to exercise your capacity for quality.

❑   ❑   ❑

❝ *Our commitment to quality is a commitment to creating products of enduring value. We believe strongly that quality and lasting value are organically linked, and that what may appear "expensive" in the short term often represents extraordinary value in the long term.* **❞**

—**Michael J. Kowalski**
President, Tiffany & Co.

◻ ◻ ◻

PHIL BERMAN

One person who has continuously clicked on *"Q"* for quality is Phil Berman. For fourteen consecutive years, he was the number one Cadillac sales professional in the nation. It stuns me when anyone achieves the rank of number one in the nation, whatever he or she does. Phil Berman's commitment, each and every day, to quality relationships, is the reason he is so successful.

Phil was born during the depression and eventually took a temporary job selling cars. He quickly demonstrated a relationship with customers which set him apart and set the leadership standard for every other person, salesman and mechanic at that dealership.

Phil rose to "number one" and held onto his title like a prize-winning athlete.

When a customer calls in with any word of concern about his or her new

Phil Berman

car, Phil drops whatever he is doing to personally drive another car to the customer. He then sends them on their way while he waits for the car to be towed or repaired. Phil's belief is, "Deal with people honestly. Be reliable and be available to your customers before, during, and after delivery. My buyers can call me in an emergency or for any service they might need. I offer a package deal — one-stop shopping. And my customers come back again and again."

Quality is the word clients use to describe Phil. Selling cars seems an accidental product of his primary mission to be a constant leader by constant reverence for the quality of his conduct. Phil Berman's attitude of customer royalty produced his lifetime career in customer loyalty.

Phil is also a community leader; his leadership has been acknowledged in a proclamation issued by the New Jersey General Assembly citing his steadfast dedication to a multitude of organizations.

❒ ❒ ❒

❝ My commitment to the automobile business I chose over 50 years ago has created a following in sales and true friends, as I have always given my best efforts to give the utmost in Quality service to my customers at all times.

I tried to make the auto industry trouble-free for the buyers, so I took the sale in steps. First, I helped in the selection of the car to fit their needs. Then, I handled the finances, the Motor Vehicle requirements, insurance; in fact, every detail.

I took all the car preparation away from the buyer to make the chore of car-buying 'fun' — thereby retaining better than 75% repeat business. That commitment to Quality mounted up over the years and enabled me to hold world titles in the huge and competitive world of auto sales.

My devotion to my customers has been recognized many times: I was awarded an Oscar at Carnegie Hall by the National Salesmasters Organization for my "Outstanding Achievements." My personal reward was enabling me to devote time and effort to many charitable organizations and to community activities.

I have always been recognized as a "professional" in the automotive industry as I always took pride in treating my customers with the dignity, sincerity, and the professionalism they deserve.

My motto was, and still is, to always be there for my customers whenever needed — always putting the quality of my service first. **55**

—**Phil Berman**

Interlude
How's The Weather Where You Are?

The blizzard of 1996 brought both beauty and pain to much of the northeast. As prisoners of the snow, many of us stayed home from the office. A writer in Cambridge, Mass. used the blizzard as a kind of litmus test to see how and if the virtual office, in home computers and faxes, could replace the traditional office environment.

The news from the information highway was pretty much what you would have expected. A vice president at Lotus described the joy of giving lunch to his daughters and then returning to his study for an afternoon of work. It sounded idyllic. No commute. The virtual workplace could be efficient, comfortable and satisfying. Ahh, what bliss . . . to be able to work and shovel snow.

After the second or third day, things started to change. The virtual office could not provide colleagues you could look at when you spoke, nor the jokes, stories, and gossip that made up daily conversation. Cabin fever was setting in. People just couldn't wait to get back to the office.

Are you the kind of colleague people would miss in a snowstorm, or someone who makes people grateful for blizzards? Imagine yourself as a meteorologist reporting on your own "internal weather." Are today's skies sunny or is there a storm brewing? Perhaps some unexpected hail at about four in the afternoon? Know your own rhythms, strengths and weaknesses. Nobody wants a Pollyanna hanging around, but neither do we want bleak, unexpected moods moving in. Keep your own weather chart. A good leader is both weather and weatherman.

❑ ❑ ❑

PART THREE

The Power Of Innovation

❐ Welcomed By The Leader

❐ Fosters Environment Of Creativity

❐ Envisions A Better Tomorrow

Those who nurture the leader within, embrace change and create an atmosphere that sparks creativity.

Leaders welcome innovation. They foster an environment which encourages creativity, welcomes new possibilities, casts aside the restrictions of the moment and envisions a better tomorrow. Innovation means the ability to do something that makes a difference. Innovators embrace change.

Pause and contemplate the basic power of innovation alive within yourself. Picture a new development that you have helped bring to life. Click on "**I**" for *innovation* and you see what happens. You need not learn how to be innovative, you have that ability. It is inherent in who you are.

AL NEUHARTH

Who else but the dynamic Al Neuharth would dare to call his memoirs *Confessions of an S.O.B?* While that might suggest an irascible spirit, I found him, throughout the course of our meetings, to have undeniable qualities of leadership. Innovation is paramount among his attributes; he led his team by thinking imaginatively.

When Al Neuharth became chairman of the Gannett Corporation, it was a modest national group comprised of small to medium-sized daily newspapers. When Al Neuharth founded *USA Today,* Gannett joined the major leagues by creating an entirely different style for a national newspaper. Al Neuharth spawned change and innovation. His leadership created jobs, bred invention, and created a tremendous new asset for his stockholders.

Al Neuharth

On two separate occasions, Al Neuharth and the former chairman of Gannett, Paul Miller, attempted to recruit me to become the publisher of their Rochester, New York newspaper. We first met at the New York State Publishers' convention held at Lincoln Hotel in Rochester. I remember it well, because they were both so persuasive. Nevertheless, I told them that my allegiance remained with the Hearst Corporation and I did not accept their offer.

My most vivid memory of that meeting was Al's clear description of the changes he envisioned for his Gannett Company. He talked about creating a nationwide newspaper company that would divide into geographic regional newspaper clusters for more focused management. He wanted to use talent banks to identify and store information about their best potential leaders, and organizational precision, the better to streamline operations by swiftly shared information. All of these concepts were unorthodox departures from most traditional newspaper companies of that time.

His description was so vivid, it was like watching him use his personal leadership brush to paint his innovations into the constantly growing landscape of his company. His leadership would motivate his associates to lift their talents to new brilliance.

Two years later, Al Neuharth touched down in Albany, on his corporate jet, with his entourage of senior colleagues, Jack Heselden, head of operations, and John Quinn, top editor.

When I met privately with Al, it hardly seemed that two years had passed since he had described his vision for Gannett. His ability to lead had been amply confirmed by the unparalleled growth of his company and the unprecedented record of year after year consecutive quarterly earning gains.

❏   ❏   ❏

His enthusiasm was palpable as he began our meeting with his description and conviction of how a new national newspaper could be positioned for a broad new reading audience. He described a generation that had grown up with the color, speed, brevity and packaging of television. These innovations he described were precise, well-formed and compelling. They even included a new newspaper sale rack designed to look like a television set on a pedestal. That vision became *USA Today*, now a permanent part of the national media landscape.

He outlined an offer for me to run Gannett's Rochester newspaper. I would also become the first senior manager responsible for the entire Northeastern group of Gannett newspapers. I explained to Al that his offer was extremely attractive but that my entire career, all the opportunities I had been afforded, had flowed from my association with the Hearst Corporation.

He looked at me very carefully and said he didn't think I could make that kind of decision alone. He thought I owed it to my family to accept Gannett's offer because they were a public company, and because the growth in their stock and other options available to me were very important to my family's future.

Again, I was deeply honored by Al Neuharth's offer. I knew that if I turned him down a second time, chances were, there would not be a third opportunity. While I felt the strongest allegiance to my family, I needed to remain loyal to the company which paved the way to my ascension as publisher of the *Albany Times Union*. I remained with Hearst.

"This is a first for me," Al said before explaining that I was the first person, outside of Gannett, whom he had attempted to recruit, and who had turned him down. He added that he would not forget my reasons for not accepting his offer.

Some years later, in February of 1977, I became the head of the Hearst newspaper group in New York City. The first phone call I received on my first day in my new office was from Al Neuharth. "Bob," he said, "I know you're there to take over the helm of the Hearst newspapers, and I want you to know that I never forgot the fact that you told me, at the time we tried to persuade you to join Gannett, that your first allegiance was to Hearst."

"That loyalty," he continued, "is a great attribute and one that's going to be a great asset for all the Hearst newspapers. I know they're going forward. That newspaper company will never be the same. It will be better — largely because of the special fidelity you bring to Hearst."

As he spoke about remembering my loyalty as the keynote in our several conversations, I reflected on the spirit of his innovation as my paramount memory of my meetings with him. When he founded *USA Today* in 1982, it became the single greatest innovation in modern newspaper history. The heavy use of process color, the jump policy for page one, the factoid information briefs, the full color weather map, the personality features, the abundant coverage of every sport, and the nationwide distribution — all became models which influenced newspaper and television paradigms throughout the world.

The Neuharth name is synonymous with innovation. His influence for change spread across the entire spectrum of newspaper publishing. Al may have saluted my loyalty to Hearst newspapers as a hallmark of our paths' crossings. His phone call of congratulations, on my first day at the helm of Hearst newspapers, was a testimony to his attention to detail. It is his innovations as a leader which left an indelible impression on me.

❝ Innovation and change are essential in the development of any business or profession. But it's important that in making those changes we preserve the best and improve the rest. ❞

—Al Neuharth

❐ ❐ ❐

CONNA CRAIG

It was the invitation to be the keynote speaker at the annual convention of the International Foster Care Professionals which set me on a course that would weave a thread of life named Conna Craig into my personal tapestry.

Although a product of the foster home system, I was not current on critical issues in foster care today. Researching those issues led me to Conna Craig — this was a gift, as her capacity for innovative leadership is touching the lives of foster care children in a profound way.

Conna was herself a foster child, one of more than 100 children taken in by Joe and Muriel Craig, a couple

Conna Craig

in Northern California. The Craigs happily adopted Conna when she was eight years old, giving her the singular joy of having a last name. Unclear about her actual birth date or ethnic roots, Conna's friends guess that she is Norwegian, Latina, Chinese or Hawaiian. Age and ethnicity are uncertainties in Conna's background.

What is certain is the richness of her intellect, which resulted in a Harvard education, and the spirited commitment she brings to her laser-focused efforts to reshape foster care and adoption in America.

Conna's honors thesis at Harvard dealt with the relationship between research and legislation on child abuse. In the course of her research, she traveled across the United States, meeting with children in foster care, group homes and shelters. She explains that she "met many children who, temporarily or permanently separated from their families of origin, languished for months or even years in state care."

From her personal experience as an adopted child who had "found a Mom," coupled with her commitment to creating policy blueprints that would tangibly improve the foster care system, Conna co-founded an organization to focus with facts and intelligence on reshaping foster care and adoption.

Conna brought to this challenge her leadership power of innovation, creating the Institute for Children, Inc. After identifying the key factors that stood in the way of foster children's securing permanent, loving homes, the Institute created strategies to restructure America's $12 billion system of public agency child welfare, a system in which more than 650,000 children will spend all or part of this year. A key strategy of the Institute for Children is to help restructure the existing child welfare funding mechanisms in order to create incentives to get children out of long-term state care and into permanent, loving homes.

Conna succeeded in demonstrating the power of innovation in 1993 to then-Governor William Weld of Massachusetts. Governor Weld responded eagerly to her proposed action plan, "What a Governor Can Do to Make Foster Care and Adoption Work." Following the implementation of that plan, the number of foster child adoptions in Massachusetts increased from 599 to 1,068 in just two years. Of course, many factors led to the increase, and the Institute for Children was a key player in the change.

Conna has taken the Massachusetts success to other governors, galvanizing change in their state foster care systems. She points to the fact that nationwide, there are more than 500,000 foster children who are free to be adopted, yet languish in the foster care system because of a bloated social service bureaucracy that fails to recruit aggressively adoptive families, or finalize adoptions in a timely manner.

Conna Craig has infused the power of innovation into the Institute for Children. The very charter she wrote for the Institute sparkles from her drive to bring permanent innovation to the entire foster care system; the mission of the Institute is to reshape foster care and adoption so that every child will have the chance to grow up in a loving, permanent family. The mission is achieved by initiating policy reforms directed not to building bigger or more expensive programs, but to caring for our most vulnerable children.

Conna was herself one of those vulnerable children. Her awareness of the "client side" of the foster care and adoption equation strengthens her commitment to ensuring that countless future foster children will have what their hearts yearn for — a Mom and Dad, and a last name.

ɑɑ *Innovative leadership requires a powerful message with a strong vision. The Institute for Children's message is universal and undeniable; children need permanent loving homes. I think that this message brings out the most generous impulses in people; I have seen families open their hearts and homes to children of all ages, of every ethnic background and with every type of disability. The Institute's vision is one of a nation in which every child has the chance to grow up in a permanent, loving family. The idea itself is not innovative; to love and care for our children is perhaps the most deeply ingrained component of who we are as human beings. Innovation comes into play in the manner by which the Institute is achieving its mission.*

Innovation requires (1) courage to challenge the status quo; (2) ability to identify solutions; and (3) willingness to help bring about those solutions.

Five years ago, I could not have imagined how much resistance to change I would encounter in the

entrenched bureaucracy of public agency child welfare. Though I am convinced that most in the field of
child welfare are committed to the well-being of children, it quickly became apparent that administrators,
researchers and practitioners were working within a
complex bureaucracy that is monolithic and slow to
change. If I have demonstrated courage in challenging this $12 billion industry, that courage comes en-
tirely from my faith in God and my understanding that
His hand is in this endeavor, helping to bring about
the changes necessary to get children home.

It is not enough to chronicle the failure of the system without offering alternatives that work. The
Institute's Private Initiative Leadership project identifies community-based, often faith-based, private-sec-
tor approaches to foster care and adoption. Its Governors' Project identifies and works with leaders in key
states, such as South Carolina and Kansas, that are
pioneering legislation and practices to shorten the time
children will spend in care, and to ensure their safety
there. The efforts of those states are innovative in that,
rather than simply calling for increased spending or
additional programs, leaders are putting into practice
strict timelines as well as privatization of foster care
and adoption; these are radical changes that have as
their goals permanency and safety for all children.

Effecting lasting change will be the key to the
Institute's ultimate success. This success can be defined only in terms of the outcomes of proposed blueprints. At the Institute we call this the "kid in Kansas"
measurement; our progress is gauged by the potential
of each of our projects to improve the life of one boy
or one girl, whose name we will never know, who will
never hear of Conna Craig or the Institute for Children, but who will have the chance to grow up knowing that he or she is loved. 🙶

—Conna Craig

RUPERT MURDOCH

Rupert Murdoch

Newspaper men may come and go, but like historic England's influence on much of the civilized world, the everlasting impact of Rupert Murdoch is here to stay. This swashbuckling innovator is the chairman of News Corp., the international media corporation. He has spent his entire career creating new businesses that have left his competitors stunned at the starting gate. In many ways, he's a thoroughbred — strong, focused, and quick.

It was Rupert Murdoch who secretly installed a revolutionary new computerized publishing system and modern presses in a remote part of a London suburb; only a few respected colleagues knew about the development. At the time, British labor unions were blamed for suffocating progress and profit of all the newspapers in England. Murdoch created highly efficient, state of the art, multi-million dollar presses which were fronted by a totally vacant modern newspaper plant. The plant was assumed vacant because Murdoch had surreptitiously built the presses so that no permanent union employees knew they were there. There was a great risk word would leak out, and his highly innovative presses would be damaged.

In a final confrontation with the once powerful unions, new employees were shipped into the plant. To the astonishment of everyone, the new high-tech plant rolled newspapers off the brand new presses and the print union environment of England was changed forever. Innovation of one leader had a permanent influence on an entire national industry.

We felt his influence in America, too. In the early 1980s, when our company was faced with the harsh reality of a failing Boston newspaper that had primitive, suffocating labor conditions, we decided that only the threat of closing the operation might cause the union leadership to change its view. We wanted them to agree to the essential contract modifications that would permit new technologies, reduce labor waste and give the newspaper the prospect of survival. We finally decided to sell. We believed that, after decades of our owning the paper, the local labor unions would not find our threat of closure credible.

After months of fruitless efforts to find a new owner for the newspaper, only Murdoch's News Corp. emerged as a prospect. Every needed labor contract change was detailed. A News Corp. team of lawyers and labor specialists spent several intense weeks negotiating, change by change, with the union leadership, until only the most difficult labor relief issues remained. That was when Rupert Murdoch arrived personally to handle the toughest part of the negotiations.

The hourglass was turned over. I was stationed with a management team at the newspaper while Rupert and his team were negotiating at a nearby hotel. It was 3:30 in the morning when Rupert called to tell me that they had exhausted all their efforts. That moment seemed to me as dark inside as it was outside. One union was intransigent and Rupert was about to tell all the unions he was heading for the airport to leave Boston for good. I asked him to wait until we made one final effort.

After checking with our company president, Frank Bennack, who was also up all night in our New York command post, I shut down the presses and evacuated the building until only I remained. Our team then left for the labor meeting room, where we were joined by Rupert's team, and a room full of the Boston media and union negotiating teams.

"It's over," we told the unions.

They all knew we had closed the plant — an action that sent shock waves. We thanked the union members for their diligent efforts to save the jobs and the newspaper, and then turned to the hold-out union leader and said, "This is the guy putting the lock on the door."

The union leader immediately asked for a private meeting with the Murdoch team and agreed to the changes that would save the day.

When the going was the toughest, Rupert Murdoch personally put himself on the line. I'll always remember his willingness to try my one more idea before closing the door of opportunity. In the final analysis, his leadership and openness to an innovative idea saved the jobs and the newspaper's unique voice.

When Rupert turned his strategic focus to the electronic and entertainment media, he brought his sweeping capacity for innovation to them. He acquired 20th Century Fox movie studio, and with breathtaking regularity, it became a house of steady box office hits.

His vision contemplated an entire new national television network. The Fox network was the result, and is now a national resource. When the new Fox network needed a major credibility infusion in order to stand as a full competitor to the long established networks, Rupert stunned the media world by outbidding CBS for the broadcast of professional football games. Overnight, his innovative vision changed the television landscape.

The history of his company, News Corp., is punctuated with affirmation that it is a major league global presence because of Rupert Murdoch's ground-breaking ideas and leadership.

REFLECTIONS ON
R U P E R T   M U R D O C H

Characteristic of INNOVATION
By: William O'Neill, Executive Vice President
Human Resources, News Corporation

*O*ne of our Australian executives once likened working for Rupert Murdoch to riding on a magic carpet. Once the journey begins, it becomes not a job, but an exciting adventure. You have no idea what challenges lie ahead or where the ride will take you.

During the past 35 years I have been fortunate to have witnessed Rupert's mission in building News Corporation into one of the world's most dynamic media organizations with a truly global spread.

I can't think of any businessman with a vision or drive that parallels Rupert's. Many of his accomplishments — from pioneering satellite broadcasting and building a fourth television network, to challenging the archaic, restrictive work practices of the British print unions — have made him unique.

❏   ❏   ❏

JOHN F. (JACK) WELCH, JR.

John F. Welch, Jr.

"Control your own destiny or someone else will," Jack Welch once said. Innovators do not wait for change to happen. On the contrary, they initiate it. They see possibilities when and where others do not.

General Electric, which Jack Welch has turned into one of the world's greatest corporations, is a good example. Founded in the late part of the nineteenth century by Thomas Edison, the inventor of the lightbulb, GE lit the way for innovation. When Jack Welch's turn came to turn on the lights in the company, he turned up the wattage so that everyone around him could see the necessity for change. "Companies can't give job security," he'd say to his employees, "only customers can."

It was while visiting my daughter, Mary Beth, and her family in Salem, Massachusetts, that I first came across the legacy of Jack

Welch. Several hundred years before I visited there, some Salem residents were thought to be possessed by witchcraft and sorcery. It was in Salem, that I, too, became aware of someone who had a gift for magic. This time, however, there was nothing to fear, unless, of course, you belonged to the competition.

I was taking an early morning walk through Salem's manicured streets when I began to contemplate a circumstance that was arising back at work. The early 1990's recessionary climate weighed heavily on our newspapers, and our advertising revenues were expected to weaken in the business cycles ahead. We needed to focus our newspaper publishers' attention on cost, without letting the guillotine and subsequent loss of morale, fall on our employees. At that moment, I passed a bookstore displaying a book about Salem's native, favorite son, Jack Welch, now chairman of the General Electric Corporation. I was curious and bought the book, *Control Your Destiny*, later that morning. The book's jacket showed a man with a twinkle in his eye. For a moment I thought he was a newspaperman because he exuded curiosity.

As I continued to read this wonderful story of how Jack Welch changed the destiny of General Electric, I realized that I needed to share this information with my associates around the nation. Welch provided exciting innovative ideas for infusing an appetite for productivity in the entire management structure of every business unit. The book inspired clear thoughts as to how we could more scientifically forecast personnel retirement and attrition. It provoked a new way of thinking — how to become increasingly more efficient while easing the employee anxiety associated with heartrending layoffs and downsizing.

The next day, my office ordered copies of *Control Your Destiny* for each of our publishers, thus launching the beginning of a corporate culture commitment to productivity. We breathed his ideas and ideals into our company, with productivity as a positive objective rather than simple cost-cutting and cost containment, because these negatives imply a lack of trust and confidence in your employees.

Jack Welch was the only child born to Grace and John Welch Sr., who praised, nurtured and loved him. John, Sr. was a conductor for the Boston and Maine railroad, who rose before daylight to spend fourteen hour days away from home. Because of this, young Jack was powerfully influenced by his mother. She taught him to be independent, self-confident and resourceful.

Armed with a Ph.D. in chemical engineering, Jack drove his Volkswagen Beetle to his first job with G.E. Plastics in Pittsfield, Mass., where one of his new colleagues was Lee Guittar, a bright communications specialist. Guittar had been a senior executive with our Hearst newspaper family for the past decade.

Jack was an innovative leader from the day he arrived in Pittsfield. The casual atmosphere of the plastics operation gave him range to nurture the unique business leadership style that has defined his career. He preached consistency of ideas, reality, agility and ownership, "Give your people every chance to identify with their business. Their enthusiasm is your most valuable asset."

□   □   □

The Jack Welch philosophy is rooted in his attitude of "change before you have to."

When he won the horse race as GE's Chief Executive Officer, observers were quick to point out his ability to change as his most winning attribute. That characteristic showed clearly in his earliest GE assignments.

As the corporation's youngest general manager of a division, he was overseeing two competing plastic products, Lexan and Noryl. Traditional GE procedure would have been to choose one product for market concentration. The innovator, young Mr. Welch, retained both products and then launched heady, inventive, first-time ever advertising campaigns for each. He used comics, Bob and Ray, for truly humorous radio commercials geared at the automobile industry — television spots which showed a bull in a china shop busting up every item, except those made with his Lexan based component. Suddenly, and for the first time, the Jack Welch plastics team saw ads about their products. This sparked a first ever team spirit among those managers. Innovation unlocked it.

A passionate advocate of having GE as number one, or at least number two in every market it served, Jack Welch forced the traditional GE to swallow his changes no matter how much they groaned. The essence of his innovation was that ideas would drive the GE revolution.

Welch believes a company without boundaries is a company setting itself up for success. Barriers of geography, function and corporate structure were meant to be challenged; companies with one set design only cut themselves off from potential partnerships and customers.

Speed, simplicity, self confidence and trust are other Jack Welch priorities. He concluded that communication within GE should not be the plant newspaper, videos or speeches. His innovation called for a new attitude that would stimulate direct person or eyeball to eyeball communication. He incorporated that concept into his meeting with his corporate executive council of 30 senior managers, who spent two full days a month in direct dialogue with him. He pushed personal communication throughout GE in the program called "work-out," where managers had direct, candid, face to face exchanges to resolve issues and identify opportunities. Slowly, but surely, every GE employee became conscious of change, of innovation, and of new ideas. He became a cheerleader, declaring "the world will belong to passionate, driven leaders, people who not only have enormous amounts of energy, but who can energize those whom they lead."

Globalization to expand the company as a world-class presence for GE business was yet another innovation. Using his "work-out" direct communication program, he infused a new world attitude into every corner of the company.

Born from his direct personal commitment to change, the direct dialogue eyeball to eyeball system of the "work-out" program, succeeded in helping Jack reach his objectives to build trust, empower employees, eliminate unnecessary work and nurture a boundaryless organization.

In early 1997, GE became America's most profitable company. This distinction is rooted in Jack Welch's innovative and unique leadership. The heart of this achievement lies in Jack's ability to make the power of potent new ideas beat a steady pulse throughout GE.

Jack Welch's leadership brought change to G.E. His leadership culture sparks profound insights like these:

☐ *Management is fine as far as it goes, but leadership is the way to win.*

☐ *We hired the arms and backs and legs of people for years, and we never knew the brains came free.*

☐ *The only way to cope with so much responsibility is to lead; management would take too much time. The leader's success depends on the ability to assemble and motivate teams of people who can accomplish tasks by themselves.*

☐ *Change has no constituency. The leader has to be prepared for resistance.*

☐ *A leader has to be hard to be soft. You must demonstrate the ability to make the hard, tough decisions if you want credibility when you promote the soft values. We did reduce employment and cut the bureaucracy, but when we spoke of soft values, of things like candor, fairness and facing reality — people listened.*

Ultimately, Jack Welch's path of leadership led him to the C.E.O. position at G.E., already one of the largest companies in the world. He didn't have a crystal ball, but he could see into tomorrow. His vision for the future mandated that G.E. refocus its world priorities and create new breakthrough products and performance standards. He was one man among multitudes of G.E. employees worldwide. He was one man staring up at a mountain of bureaucratic comfort developed over decades. He was one man prepared to make every minute of every day productive. Through his innovative leadership, Jack Welch ensured G.E.'s position as a world leader. Innovation is a bit like alchemy, and Jack Welch was able to take that which lacked luster at G.E. and turn it into gold.

REFLECTIONS ON
JACK WELCH

Characteristic of INNOVATION
By: Lee J. Guittar, Hearst Newspaper Group Executive

During our early days together in Pittsfield, Mass., I knew Jack Welch mostly by reputation. We were assigned to different segments of the Company, but a friend and associate who worked in Employee Relations at G.E. Plastics, brought tales to our plant-wide meetings of a new, young tiger at work in what was then a tiny component of the General Electric Company. From the perspective of someone working closely with Jack, he described him as brilliant, hotly competitive, intolerant of unnecessary restraints a bureaucracy would put in his way and afire with innovation.

Naturally, his young associates cheered him on. Older associates were not equally enthusiastic about his aggressive approach to solving problems. But all recognized the power of leadership, accomplishment, determination to succeed and spirit for change which he bought to every assignment.

Years later, a senior G.E. executive told me that Jack brought that same determination to the golf course: "He doesn't putt the ball into the hole. He wills it in!"

Some 25 years later, Jack and I found ourselves together, playing in the same Pro-Am golf tournament. He was already C.E.O. of the General Electric Company. I was then Publisher of The Denver Post. We reminisced about our Pittsfield days, with Jack saying that he remembered me "as a big shot;" (I was the plant spokesman, and got my name in the paper frequently), and my remembering him as a young man with a flaming appetite for innovation. My memory was more accurate than his!

Twenty-five years later, he is still innovating . . . but despite the years and the pace at which he has traveled, he is still a "regular guy," down-to-earth and fun to be around. Jack Welch is truly a great role model for aspiring Chief Executive Officers.

◻ ◻ ◻

LELAND STANFORD

It seems to me, institutions begin with an individual's vision, combining idea, ambition and prospect. When fulfilled, that institution can have a permanent influence.

A leader leaves footprints that are not only accessible to those who cross his path, but to those who choose to follow decades or centuries later. In that way, the leader's map of accomplishments is akin to the archaeologist's.

As I stood for the first time in the magnificent scholastic quad of Stanford University, as one of twelve national Professional Journalism Fellowship winners, I was awed by the balance and the beauty of the place. My first day there, I came across a bronze plaque describing the accomplishments of the university's founder, Leland Stanford. A former governor of California and former senator, he was the founder of the first transcontinental railroad that linked East to West.

Leland Stanford, Jr.

Stanford was born to a farm family in Watervliet, New York, just outside the capital city of Albany. I was stunned because I had lived with a foster family in that same small town of Watervliet. Although Leland Stanford walked those upstate New York streets more than one hundred years before I was born, we had, more than likely, set our footprints on some of the very same avenues. After the passing of the generations, we were linked again by virtue of my having the unique opportunity to walk the pathways of the great university that reflected the innovational leadership of the man. My footsteps touched the ground where he was born, and the ground that bore the gift of his leadership.

In November, 1769, the Spanish explorers camped under a towering redwood tree as they prepared to venture forth to explore San Francisco bay. The hundred foot tall redwood became a landmark for explorers, missionaries and soldiers as they traveled the peninsula which they named Palo Alto, or "high tree." When the successful railroad builder, Leland Stanford, developed his stock farm near San Francisco, to raise thoroughbred horses, he adopted the name Palo Alto for his farm, which included that majestic tree.

Leland and Jane Stanford had one son, Leland, Jr. Slender, studious and at fifteen, taller than his father's five feet ten, he had accompanied his family to Italy where he contracted typhoid fever. On March 13, 1884, Leland, Jr. died in Florence, a few weeks shy of his sixteenth birthday. His father, then Governor of California, remained at the boy's side continuously and fell into a troubled sleep the morning his son died.

When he awoke and learned of the tragic loss of his only son, he turned to his wife and said, "the children of California shall be our children." With those words, he began the journey which would lead him to create and dedicate Stanford University in perpetual memory of his son.

Leland Stanford did not only endow the proposed new college financially; he searched for the very best in educational innovation to model as his gift to the children of California.

He traveled to Cornell, Yale and Harvard to understand better what made them exemplary educational institutions. He engaged Frederick Law Olmstead, the eminent landscape architect who designed New York's Central Park, to bring creativity to those Palo Alto lands. He pursued the gifted Ph.D., David Starr Jordan, and persuaded him to move from the University of Indiana, where he had been the architect of great educational advances, to California. Legend has it, that he walked Doctor Starr to the majestic redwood tree on his Palo Alto farm and challenged him to build a university of intellectual majesty to match that mighty tree. He challenged him to bring fresh perspectives and new educational horizons to the campus to be named Stanford.

That tall tree is the centerpiece of the University's seal. It has historic significance and symbolizes the strength, independence and enduring qualities a university must possess. It is also a symbol of the leadership of a single man, Leland Stanford, whose innovative vision created a world of knowledge and opportunity from a single tree.

The thousands who enter the quiet solemnity of Stanford's main academic quadrangle can read the plaque about a man whose first footprints in Watervliet, New York, created the pathway to Stanford university, an educational jewel renowned for its ongoing commitment to innovation.

I believe all institutions and organizations in our great nation can trace their beginnings to some individual exercising leadership. Innovation is a natural gift within us, which each of us has the opportunity to nurture in order to bring out our leader within.

REFLECTIONS ON
LELAND STANFORD

Characteristic of INNOVATION
By: Gerhard Casper, President, Stanford University

*U*niversities are often gauzily portrayed as "the halls of ivy," and, indeed, tradition is important to these, and all, institutions. However, the most important university tradition is antithetical to the static image of ivy-covered walls. It is the central value of the search for knowledge, of questioning and challenging fundamental assumptions and practices and, by implication, of favoring change if these assumptions and practices prove to be wrong.

By its very nature, the true university is the ally of change — in other words, innovation. And by the very nature of innovation, the true university exhibits leadership.

The tradition that Jane and Leland Stanford established in their university added a "Western" spirit of pioneering, entrepreneurship and energy. While ivy can be found on the Stanford campus, it is not the dominant plant. The faculty and students of Stanford University benefit from, and continue, the leadership of the university's founders. Examples range from Paul Berg's work with DNA, which spawned the field of genetic engineering, to John Chowning's work in signal generation, which was the foundation for music synthesizers; from exploration in the humanities and social sciences to manifold contributions to the Silicon Valley, and from service to the community to athletic excellence.

David Starr Jordan, Stanford's first president, suggested to Leland Stanford a motto for the young institution: "Die Luft der Freiheit weht" ("The wind of freedom blows"). In Jordan's words, "Mr. Stanford was impressed with the winds of freedom — which we hoped would continue to blow over Stanford University . . . " Those winds of freedom do, indeed, continue to blow, and to bring with them the fresh air of innovation. Through their creation of Stanford University, Jane and Leland Stanford established a self-perpetuating legacy of leadership and innovation.

❑ ❑ ❑

Interlude
Get Out And Lead

For a moment, pause to think of a very interesting four letter word — *goal*. In a sport such as hockey, your objective is to get your puck into your opponent's goal as often as possible, while, conversely trying to keep the opposing team from scoring. Offense and defense change hands rapidly to create a never ending game of speed, skill, talent and determination. Whoever gets the most goals wins.

In football, a field goal sailing perfectly through the goal posts can be a breathtaking sight for the sports fan — even though a slower, more pensive element of the game. The test for the team now includes a reality check — a more realistic goal if you will — by not asking your kicker to attempt a goal from too far a distance.

Outside of sports, you can be successful while trying to achieve your goals; getting on the right path is just part of the game plan. Once you're on track, one goal leads you to another, until you're at the apex of achievement.

As defined in the *Oxford English Dictionary*, a goal is "the object of one's ambition or effort, an end or result towards which behavior is consciously or unconsciously directed." Ambition and effort are parts of the qualities of leadership which can be flushed out by very conscious behavior. To be fully conscious is to be aware of every moment; it is to be alert and open, mentally and physically, to all possibilities. Leadership is, by definition and implication, heightened consciousness.

❏   ❏   ❏

PART FOUR

The Power Of Inspiration

❏ To Inspire Is To Impart A Gift

❏ Touches Spirit With Richness Of Messages

❏ As Simple As Appreciation

When you hear the word inspiration, do you think of the definition that has to do with guidance and influence, or do you remember its root meaning — to breathe upon or into? Breath goes through the body and keeps the whole system alive and functioning. To inspire someone is to impart a gift as essential as breath.

Each of us have been inspired by people who have motivated us to move with enthusiasm on the pathways we have chosen to pursue. Leaders take time to check out all the options on their pathways. They clarify the value of their direction and encourage others to join and not just follow them. Leaders touch our spirit with the richness of their message in order to absorb the shocks on the roads ahead. They appreciate the individual and acknowledge that each possesses worth and counts in making the ride less bumpy. Leaders know value and how to translate such a simple concept into a larger vision.

NELSON ROCKEFELLER

Nelson Rockefeller was a colorful, outspoken politician and a visionary when he was governor of New York. He, too, ignited the leader within; his legacy connects New York in the same way that railroad tracks criss-cross the nation, connecting larger cities to smaller ones, the north to the south, and metropolitan areas to rural towns. He inspired people to embrace his dreams and drew others to join him in the development of those dreams.

Nelson Rockefeller

He was a true kindler and pathmaker — a trail blazer. He had the inspiration to create the prestigious SUNY state university system and a greatly enhanced statewide highway system. Governor Rockefeller inspired others to help make his visions reality. He was also a big enough man to allow others to inspire him. In turn, he would channel that inspiration into other people.

It was Governor Rockefeller who saw the possibility of a state capital presence, the Empire Plaza, which would inspire pride in state employees and visitors to Albany. Although the beneficial impact of the project on the city of Albany was immense, the Governor's version of a new downtown, complete with government offices, did have some flaws. Originally called the South Mall, the enormous project, with its magnificent architecture and sweeping scope, covered a vast downtown area. Gleaming marble would replace the faded Albany core, the way cartoonists often picture the new year replacing the previous one at the stroke of midnight. Planning was precise and professional; everything about the South Mall project would inspire awe and admiration. Once a person encountered that inspiring architecture, mind, body and soul would be elevated. The design appeared flawless.

However, in the assessment of our newspapers, The *Albany Times Union* and *Knickerbocker News*, a gaping flaw persisted when that same person stood in the neighborhoods outside the South Mall. Newspaper reporters examined in detail the living conditions for the large population whose homes were now in its shadow. Editorials began to appear that urged the state government to include those decaying neighborhoods as part of the Albany renaissance. What good is a flawless diamond if set in the rough? How can you have marble facades when the houses of neighboring buildings are crumbling? Why didn't the blueprints pick up on the necessity of considering the human factor in the landscape?

After the reporting and editorial writing had gained momentum, the Governor asked me to join him for lunch to discuss the newspaper's accounts and comments. Aside from a few pleasantries, he went straight to his point and said he was terribly disappointed with the negative spin our newspapers were putting on this most important initiative designed to benefit the very city our newspapers were housed in. He said it was outrageous for us to place the spotlight on the surrounding neighborhoods since the heart of the project was the new state office building complex. He said he was certain I would see his point if we could only talk it through. I said he might very well be right, but that I would make one request.

"Of course," he replied.

I told him, "I would like to continue the discussion in the back seat of your chauffeured car while I give your driver directions."

He found this a peculiar request but agreed. With that, we set off and wound our way through the slums that bordered the South Mall project. A Rockefeller, a limousine and I traveled through neglected, half-abandoned neighborhoods with the State building hovering over us like a guilty conscience. I pointed to the rundown homes and said that each morning the people living in these dreadful circumstances would step outside their homes, look up in any direction, and see a sight like Oz. Then, they would look at their paths to this magnificence and see it littered with broken homes and lost dreams. These people would conclude that their lives would go on untouched by the great changes emerging before their eyes. After a few minutes of silence, the Governor told me he had never traveled this way before.

When we returned to the driveway of the Governor's mansion, I turned to him and said that our newspapers were thrilled he had chosen Albany as the site of what would be the most striking state office complex in the nation; I said it was an absolute gem. But, I added, to ignore the surrounding neighborhoods in the restoration was to place that jewel in a cesspool! He repeated that exact phrase to me — a jewel in a cesspool.

I explained that our newspapers' efforts to spotlight the issue were really designed to cause his administration to see the necessity and the opportunity to do a truly complete job; to create the South Mall and give promise to a whole new downtown Albany, while simultaneously developing the housing, parks and amenities for the surrounding neighborhoods. This would give equal promise to all those people who had been left behind.

We left each other with a cordial handshake while he murmured the phrase of the day, "a jewel in a cesspool." The next day, he announced a new neighborhood commission for the South Mall project. He inspired the commission to enlarge the boundaries of the initiative so it included upgrades of the surrounding neighborhoods; he inspired the design of the jewel's setting to maximize its shine.

Nelson Rockefeller's inspiration was open-minded and susceptible to new growth. Your leadership instinct for inspiration is the same, a natural capability that you can encourage in yourself.

REFLECTIONS ON
N E L S O N   R O C K E F E L L E R

Characteristic of INSPIRATION
By: David Rockefeller, Remembering My Brother

 was a great admirer of my older brother, but also understood that Nelson could sometimes act in ways that could be perceived as thoughtless and motivated by political calculations. However, I feel that one of Nelson's great-

est qualities was his ability to learn, and, in fact, to admit that he may not have had all the facts when he made the initial decision. It was that capacity to learn from his mistakes, to avoid being doctrinaire in his actions, that placed Nelson in a different category from most of his contemporaries.

There is an ancillary aspect of this capacity to learn from one's mistakes; to keep one's word. I traveled with Nelson in Latin America during the late 1940s and early 1950s, when Nelson was just starting IBEC and its not-for-profit counterpart, the American International Association for Economic and Social Development. I recall a number of times, often in small towns and villages that Nelson had visited during World War II, when the whole population turned out to greet him; not because he was an American millionaire, although that may have played a part, but because he was perceived as a man who kept his word and who would follow through on his promises and projects in the area of economic development. I think the story about him and Bob Danzig driving through the poorer sections of Albany illustrates both of these qualities.

❏ ❏ ❏

TED TURNER

Ted Turner was a guest at one of our corporate group luncheons for senior management. I sat across from him while he spoke about the future global implications of the media. As he talked about large scale issues, his eyes gleamed. It was as if the old lightbulb of inspiration was going off inside of him. He also looked mischievous; his demeanor reflected fun and accomplishment. It was obvious Ted Turner became vibrant when the conversation turned to the world of ideas — both present and future. He shared his ideas about good luck, good instincts and good leadership.

Ted Turner

Ted Turner has been described by some as "THE" media magnate of the age. Some say he has even defined the age. His accomplishments reflect his leadership and his inherent ability to bring inspiration to his associates. No matter where one travels, from Bombay to Berlin, one can turn on the television set and find CNN. He has given the world a true sense of community and immediacy, an idea which came out of his own unique vision. Through his accomplishments, Ted Turner has become a national icon.

Although successful, he did not start out with a bright light over his head predicting his future. His leadership qualities were hidden until necessity caused them to be activated. Twenty-four years old, and only a neophyte salesman with his father's nondescript billboard company, Ted Turner had to face the unexpected death of his father and the surprising fact that his father had sold the major assets of his own company. Others might have walked away from the situation, but Ted Turner turned his bad-luck inside out; he began to turn his life and the life of the company around. He inspired bankers to back him, and was able to spin what was once his father's modest business, into a successful billboard company.

To quote his biographers, Robert Goldberg and Gerald Jay Goldberg, "There were forces like gale winds at his back." Ted Turner could not save his father, but he could save his company. He was smart and energetic; a bulldozer of determination. His inspiring leadership motivated his sales force to new heights. He showed a deft understanding of the use of both the carrot and the stick. He was generous with his sales force and, early on, he was proven to be an inspirational leader.

Originating from billboards which coupled word with image, Ted Turner added sound when he purchased a small radio station.

He charmed bankers in Chattanooga, Tennessee, in 1968, into backing him, to further his exploration into the media.

When his first television station in Atlanta was struggling for survival, he said, "I just love it when people say I can't do something. There's nothing that makes me feel better, because all my life people said I wasn't going to make it."

He brought to his Georgia TV station five priorities: programming, personnel, promotion, penetration and profile. The station soon became the home station of the Atlanta Braves, with a rich mix of movies programmed around the games. He then made the single station regional by contracts with cable companies outside the Atlanta area for microwave regional delivery. In 1974 he embraced early satellite delivery, and, suddenly, his single TV station was available all over the country. With each step, he inspired others to join him in these hard new untested initiatives.

He applied his business instincts and leadership skills when the heart of his station, the Atlanta Braves, threatened to leave Atlanta. His solution was to buy the baseball team and commit to making it a world class winner.

While sailing with some friends in the spring of 1978 he asked, "What would you guys think if you could turn on your TV any time of the day or night and find out what is happening in the world?" He then went on to outline a format of four discreet half-hour segments of current events, sports, features and business news. He envisioned the use of a satellite for delivery everywhere. In a gesture to show how committed he was to the project, and to encourage support of cable owners, he said he would call it "Cable News Network." Thus, CNN was born.

Ted Turner, a competitive, highly imaginative leader, was also a visionary who saw the potential impact and rewards of satellite delivered television programming. Those who joined him in the early visionary days of developing those now household-word successes were drawn to him by the inspiration of his leadership. Business plans, marketing and product initiatives had to be developed to create the entities which would have such a national impact. Ted Turner had to bring the organizational and developmental skills to those embryonic ideas in order to mature them. Of course, Ted Turner used the leader within by clinging to all the qualities which a leader exudes. Above all, his leadership continually inspired investors, employees and partners to engage his vision. There was a crossroad in every such alliance with Ted Turner that was, at its core, a sharing of the inspiration he had for his vision. Leaders such as Turner understand inspiration's life partnership with success.

❏   ❏   ❏

❝ It's hard to be a leader unless you have some kind of passion for something. I mean, which direction are you leading in? There are all kinds of leaders. There are religious leaders who are trying to get people to be more religious and more decent in their daily lives. There are educational leaders who are trying to press for education. There are leaders in media who are trying to get their companies to make more money. So, it depends on what you're in.

Inspiration and passion usually go together. If you are going to try to persuade others to go with you, it certainly doesn't hurt that you've got very strong convictions about where you are going. Like Columbus did, for instance, to discover the New World. And, if you've got passion and conviction, you're more likely to be inspiring. If you're inspired yourself and you're passionate about something, you're more likely to succeed at it, and you're more likely to get others to come with you.

Most leaders do use their capacity to inspire others, but there's nothing wrong with being a follower. If there were no followers, there'd be nobody for leaders to lead! ❞

—Ted Turner

BOB MYERS

I had no romantic notion of going to sea, like the kind you might read about in a novel by Melville or Hemingway. My reasons were practical. When I graduated from the Naval Radio Training School in Bainbridge, Maryland, I chose a duty station aboard the U.S.S. Recovery, ARS 43, a medium-size ship dedicated to rescue and salvage missions. It had been docked for several years at the Brooklyn Navy yard, just 150 miles from my hometown of Albany, New York. It sounded like my kind of ship.

After my graduation leave, I walked across the gangplank of the Recovery, ready to use my newly learned skills as a third class radioman. As I set foot on board, the ship foghorn blared out three bursts, the gangplank rose behind me, and the U.S.S. Recovery began to pull away from the dock. This startled me; the very last thing I thought might happen in choosing this assignment was, that I would leave the cozy safety of the Brooklyn dock, and head out to points unknown, in a dark and mysterious ocean. All my other shipmates were excited by the prospect of going to sea, but this new sailor felt like a fish out of water.

From there it was all downhill. After living in a reasonably comfortable barrack at radio school, I was wholly unprepared for the stark reality of having to make my home two decks below the main ship deck, on a single piece of taut canvas, with all my belongings stored in a tiny locker.

When I heard we were going to Argentina, I brightened a bit. I imagined the warm climate would change my sullen disposition. Soon after, I learned that our destination was Argentia, Newfoundland, where we were to patrol the vast, frozen ocean all the way up to Labrador. So much for Rio!

My first memory of arriving in Newfoundland consists of piling on the foul weather gear from head to toe before venturing on deck to the icy blasts. The ship was encased in ice. Even our flag and sails looked like glass. I felt totally isolated, unable to imagine what was waiting for us beyond the dark horizon. Isolation and the stress that accompanied it made all of us feel disconnected from life as we hibernated in this lonely village. Each day was just like the one before.

It could have been a barren prison, except for the humor, mischievousness, unity of purpose, and certain rich relationships that such lonely isolation can sometimes encourage.

Above the narrow strip of canvas that served as my bedroom, was an exact duplicate canvas strip occupied by one of the ship's quartermasters, Bob Myers. A graduate of New York University, who loved great works of literature, Bob was a refined, cultured and manly person who happened to be a sailor. His calm, deliberate way brought a soothing presence to his every activity aboard the Recovery. He was a soft-spoken but commanding leader who inspired respect and allegiance from those he touched with his low-key self-assurance.

When the roughest of seas on the darkest of nights tossed us about, Bob Myers was asked to man the wheel and guide us. He did not order or coerce. He advised and requested, so that each of us was inspired to do his part in bringing order to nature's chaos and turbulence.

◻ ◻ ◻

Aboard ship, Bob Myers guided me through many great novels, coaxing me to weave my way into the nuances of character, plot and writing style, which he knew so well.

He also let his natural instinct to lead, through inspiration, flow freely to all of his shipmates who took comfort in knowing that Bob Myers was at the wheel on the most severe of our stormy days. This capacity to inspire was in him. He fine-tuned it, like a radio signal, until we could all hear it without any interference.

Later on, as my business life embraced greater opportunities to manage and exercise my own leadership, I included an emphasis on inspiration, because my memory was alive from the example of Bob Myers' gripping the massive wooden wheel of our ship, inspiring us with his calm.

All of our lives visit turbulence at some point. The leader who chooses to inspire reduces the impact of that turbulence and brings safe passage to those who join the journey.

REFLECTIONS ON

L E A D E R S H I P   T R A I T S

Characteristic of INSPIRATION
By: John H. Dalton
Secretary of the Navy

A leader is trusted. A leader takes the initiative. "Carpe Diem," Latin for "seize the day," has always been a fundamental tenet of leadership.

Good judgment is also critical to good leadership. Good judgment is not just evident in success; it can be most evident in defeat and disappointment.

A leader speaks with authority. A leader needs to have sufficient confidence in what he is saying, so that potential followers will be convinced. The best way to convince people is to speak with authority. If that authority is matched by knowledge, then the chances for successful leadership are greatly enhanced.

A leader strengthens others. A good leader does not seek to impose his or her own attitudes or solution on others. Rather, the leader provides the support and guidance that prompts others to have confidence in their own abilities and decision-making.

55

A leader remains optimistic and enthusiastic. To lead effectively, see the glass as half-full, not half-empty. Believe, every morning, that things are going to be better than before. Attitudes are infectious. Optimism and enthusiasm overcome the greatest challenges.

A leader never compromises absolutes. Defense of American freedom and obedience to the Constitution of the United States are two absolutes the Naval Service lives by and for which our sailors and marines may face death.

❑ ❑ ❑

Father Matthew Conlin

My matriculation as an evening division student at Siena College began with a probationary acceptance and concluded with an honors degree. That passage through intellectual territory was stimulated by many superb scholar teachers. Among them, Father Matthew Conlin was a triumvirate of inspiration to me as a teacher, as an administrator and as an inspirational leader.

As a Franciscan Shakespearean scholar at the college, he was such an inspiring teacher that his class always overflowed into the hallways. Students were satisfied just to listen to him over the speaker system without seeing him. His was a magical message that inspired a passionate, lasting interest in Shakespeare.

Father Matthew went on to become President of the college for several years, during which time I served as a Board Trustee. He brought that

Father Conlin

56

same inspiration to the administration of the school. He set high standards and was spontaneous in giving gratitude to those who helped achieve them. All who were touched by his radiance were motivated to do as well as possible while working with him.

Father Matthew ultimately withdrew from the presidency. Instead of returning to the classroom, he accepted an assignment to work in a Franciscan soup kitchen to feed the poor. His every action was a permanent new source of inspiration to all who knew him.

Those who choose to nurture the leader within are aware of and delighted with their roles as the sources of inspiration for their associates. They are aware of the spiritual responsibility they have to ignite the imagination and aspirations of those who look to them for leadership.

The task at hand, whatever it may be, is simply an opportunity to use that moment for the inspiration of others. That capacity to inspire is in the person, not the assignment.

❐ ❐ ❐

❝ It is true. Some leaders will inspire, form and shape those whom they lead. There are others who, as pure power figures, may command and control others, but they will neither inspire them nor influence them. Seldom will they touch them deeply.

Simply having power and responsibility does not make a real leader. I suspect that the real value of the many relationships you have created lies in the fact that you have influenced others, not merely commanded them, and in the fact that they in turn will be leaders who can influence and inspire other people.

We have a responsibility to hew out of ourselves the mature adults. When Jesus tells us to be "perfect," I am quite sure that He means that if we have made the most of the very singular and never-to-be-

duplicated, personalities, brains and emotional networks that we have received; in short, if we have done our best with what he gave us, then we are indeed "perfect." The point is, that to do all this, we often need inspiration and assistance.

Good leaders give us both. 🙶🙶

—Father Matthew Conlin, OFM

Interlude
Have You Seen Shakespeare?

Institutions have souls which consist of their purpose and objective, as well as their ability to harness creative capabilities, aspects and talents. Their souls are usually about allowing the poetry of life to seep into the organization rather than just simply uttering the words of life. Their souls are about the relationships of people. Their souls indicate whether the beauty and mystery of Shakespeare are alive in the organization in contrast to simple protocol — merely basic discourse with people that nullifies relationships.

Organizations with souls value relationships and reflect the human dynamics of understanding that we just don't hire a hand, we hire a person with all sorts of baggage, aspirations, dreams and capabilities. They have the room to house the human dimensions of people rather than just their number. I believe that if you are not open to the responsibility you have to cultivate the soul of an organization, then you diminish the capacity of your organization. To lead, or not to lead, are always the questions you must ask.

If the leader isn't conscious of the soul of an organization, isn't open to it, isn't cultivating it, then the opportunity for the followers to exercise their own inclinations and instincts in those directions are, if not aborted, limited. I don't think people with managing responsibilities have to come into an institution everyday and say, "today, I am going to do these things for the soul of the organization." They just need to be aware that if they manage the organization without the infusion of what makes the organization beautiful, it will never achieve its fullest potential.

An organization's beauty can have different forms. You can have beauty of financial performance and new product development, of new markets created and new talent opportunities. There's a lot of beauty included in these. If the sterile concept of managing the organization without emphasis on soul is the objective, then I offer up, for contemplation, the fact that the effects of this on the organization may limit the infusion of value of beauty into the organization.

One of the things that creates beauty is the celebration of success. That has to be part of your consciousness. If all you do is deal with failure, then you're not stimulating your associates' satisfaction that can come from acknowledged success. Whether it's a poem you write, or Lee Iacocca designing the Ford Mustang, what you do only matters, aside from the personal satisfaction you get from doing it, when you receive applause. Leaders have to be open to the celebration of success by applauding success. Those who do so usually operate with a sense of both spirit and zest. Welcome Shakespeare to your stages.

PART FIVE

The Power Of Perseverance

☐ Leaders Press On

☐ Hurdles Await Solutions

☐ Motivate Others To Go The Distance

L eaders have the power of perseverance. By pushing on, they inspire their colleagues to do the same and to go the extra distance. They find solutions to the hurdles before them.

ROBERT SCOTT PATTERSON

Imagine a son of slaves in Virginia, a man with little formal education, just enough to know the basics. Now imagine him walking five miles to school and another five miles from his shanty to where his family picked potatoes.

Imagine that this man marries the daughter of slaves. They find a way to go North, because the only work available to them in the South is potato picking. With hundreds of others, they stand in line outside the offices of the *Newark Evening News* and wait for the first copies of the paper, so they can search the help wanted ads. They apply for a position as a domestic couple, are hired and live in a finished basement. For several years, with the dream of being in business for themselves someday, they save every dime they can; they want some influence on the destiny which has never before been in their own hands. Now, imagine they save up enough money and buy a car.

Robert Patterson

The day Robert "Scotty" Patterson, bought that first car, he went into the transportation business. He had little signs made up reading "Scotty's Transportation," put them on the sides of the car, and dedicated himself to quality service in whatever he did. Eventually, this son of slaves built a business of several dozen cars, with as many drivers. This provided the income to allow the drivers who chose to send their children, as well as Scotty's children, to college.

Scotty is in his eighth decade today and personally drives only a few clients. As one of his few personal accounts, whenever I arrive home in a snowstorm, two or three hours late, I see Scotty waiting at the airport gate for me. Reacting to my surprise at finding him there, he always says the same thing, "Mr. Danzig, in our business you are on the case or you are not on the case."

If you care about quality service to your customers, then you are on the case; you persevere. I found this to be a profound lesson, because so many people in business, with an opportunity to exercise leadership only need to be on the case. In addition to using whatever gifts they have, that's all they have to do.

Scotty didn't have many advantages; he certainly doesn't have an MBA. He is just a man who believed he could someday control his own destiny by committing himself to be "on the case." Imagine that!

ITZHAK PERLMAN

In life, there are rare situations which are sparked by the simple presence of an unusual person. Moments such as these may not always be as intimate as those situations where we are truly, literally or personally, touched. Listening to Itzhak Perlman one night was such a moment.

Itzhak Perlman, violin virtuoso, lost the use of his legs when he was four years old, as the result of poliomyelitis. But by the age of ten, he had given numerous public concerts in Israel and made his professional debut in the United States at Carnegie Hall. His knowledge of 18th and 19th century violin repertoire is unparalleled. He has earned his international reputation as a master musician and has frequently been cited for his rich tone and flawless virtuosic technique.

Itzhak Perlman

At the concert, from the moment he appeared on stage, until the moment he exited after his final ovation, I was one of the thousands at the Lincoln Center who were mesmerized by his presence. When the theater dimmed to signal the start of the performance, in the complete silence of Avery Fisher Hall, the first sound I heard was the tap of his crutches against the floor. It was a sound that preceded the music, much as a metronome provides a beat to a musician. The audience roared its appreciation from the moment his crutch touched the stage in anticipation of his gift of music.

Perhaps I was more receptive to his gift because of my own experiences with such a person. Shortly before the concert, my wife Pat and I visited our daughter, Marsha, who has so heroically handled her own physical challenges. On the night of the concert,

I couldn't help but reflect on everyday heroes, like Marsha and Itzhak Perlman, who arrange to live their lives by cheerfully choosing to share whatever affirmative gifts they have with others. Although they are both people with greater physical challenges than most, they have no disability of spirit. They are models of perseverance.

Pat and I feel the ongoing lifetime gift we have every day by the way Marsha chooses to live her life. She graduated from Harvard, and the Sorbonne, and is now a Ph.D. candidate at Columbia University. Her worldly accomplishments reflect the triumph of her heart and soul.

At the Lincoln Center, one of the great violinists of all time had a similar impulse and inclination as Marsha to reach inside and find the ways in which he could live his life in a persevering manner, while at the same time enriching and elevating the spirit of all those who heard the magic lingering on the kiss of his violin strings. Marsha makes a different music. Those who witness the way she chooses to live her life are also filled with realization of their own possibilities.

Both Marsha Danzig and Itzhak Perlman have persevered to live their lives to the fullest. They are people with a special challenge, not disabled people. Although Itzhak Perlman performs to standing ovations and thunderous applause, while Marsha does not, both have persevered in their own lives. They are a shining example to others.

Leaders use their perseverance. They endure. They lead others with the melody of their personal music.

◻ ◻ ◻

MAX GOLDSTEIN

When I got my first job as the office boy at the *Albany Times Union*, I was also working part-time at a fruit and vegetable stand owned by Max Goldstein. Now that I think of it, Max never took his hat off either.

Though Max hadn't finished grade school, he was an eloquent, compelling speaker. His dream was actually to be as educated as he sounded. During the time I worked for him as a young teenager, he would arrive at the wholesale market by 5:00am, work all day in the store and then attend high school in the evening. After receiving his degree, he went to Siena College at night for six years, while continuing to run his fruit and vegetable stand during the day. After he received his college degree, he went on to Albany Law School. After more than a dozen years spent obtaining the education he sought, he passed the bar examination and certified that he was now as educated as he sounded.

Max Goldstein

When Max became a lawyer, he rented a storefront on the main artery, State Street, in Albany. One stormy November day, when I was traveling home from work, the bus came to a grinding halt on State Street, directly in front of Max's storefront office. The entire store window read "Maxwell E. Goldstein: Attorney-at-Law." He proudly filled his window with his name and accomplishment. The man sitting at my side on the bus, turned to me and said, "Would you look at that sign? Have you ever seen anything more ostentatious?"

I looked at him and said, "That's not showing off. That's his reward for working so long, so consistently and so hard."

My bus seat companion seemed to warm physically as I told him the story of Max. Today, I can see that Max was celebrating his capacity for perseverance with those enormous storefront signs. That perseverance enabled him to continue to become more than he was. Max Goldstein was a living testimony of the value of perseverance to all who crossed his path.

As a young teenager in his shadow, Max's dedication to perseverance registered within me; it lit my way through college and became a fundamental tenet of my business career. Years later, the memory of his step-by-step progress was a steady source of inspiration as I matriculated through Siena College every night for five years.

REFLECTIONS ON

M A X   G O L D S T E I N

Characteristic of PERSEVERANCE
By: Barbara Goldstein Cohen, Max Goldstein's Daughter

My memory is rich with the presence of my father working with me on my school lessons, because I know he was learning at the same time. When we would go to bed at night, he would read our books from beginning to end. He did this with all of our schoolbooks, so it became his education as well as ours. He learned languages that way; he learned French, Spanish and Latin.

When he went to Siena College, he would get up at 5:00 in the morning, go to Market, work all day, and then go to college at night. When he went to Albany Law School, he would get up at 5:00 in the morning, go to Market or the produce store, go to school (which at that time I think was until 1:00pm), then go back to work for the rest of the day and study in the evenings.

I was always very proud of him, and the family was always so proud of his diligence; he had always wanted to be a lawyer. Coming from a very poor family, and being a very poor boy, he married early and had children. There was no way for *him to pursue his personal dream, until the point in his life when he was in his late thirties and could start college.*

The model of his perseverance became part of me, and, as a result, I don't think I have ever started anything that I can't finish. He gave me the gift of a lifetime of personal confidence.

❑ ❑ ❑

LEE IACOCCA

The Knights of Malta is the single most prestigious organization in the Catholic Church to which a layman can be nominated. In order to be nominated, you need to be put forward by a Bishop. In 1971, I was so honored by Bishop Broderick of Albany.

We went down to St. Patrick's Cathedral in Manhattan for the investiture. For the ceremony, I was given a long, plush, velvet cloak to wear, and a large, glistening Maltese cross. Suddenly, in this costume, I felt a part of history, of all those who had come before me to receive this honor. We all received our robes and crosses, then lined up single file and were guided into the Cathedral.

Suddenly, I became aware of two dozen trumpets, sounding out triumphantly for our procession. Before that march, while being fitted with a cloak and a cross, I looked around the room and saw these giants of Catholicity from all across the country. They all looked Italian and Irish to me, and

Lee Iacocca

I was a very Jewish-looking guy, even though I had an Irish mother. I felt so out of place. As I walked through the doors of St. Patrick's,

67

under the blare of the horns, my only thought was that all the people gathered in the cathedral were going to look up and say, "Who is that impostor?" Those thoughts made me feel nervous and out of place.

After walking down the aisle of the cathedral, we knelt in the pews. My arms were shaking slightly out of apprehension at being the focus of the crowd's attention; the people there could have assumed I had borrowed the robe and cross and crashed their ceremonial march.

The man kneeling next to me kept eyeballing me with concern, until he finally leaned over, patted me on the arm and whispered, "relax, it's just another day." All it took was one person, the words of one man, and I was fine. I spotted him afterwards at the reception and went up to him to thank him. Because his words had such a calming effect on me, I was able to relax and enjoy the majesty of the day.

"I just want to thank you very much for calming me down," I said. I was a bit anxious. "By the way, my name's Bob Danzig."

"It's nice to meet you," he said, "My name is Lee Iacocca."

Whenever I read about his achievements and think about what he did to infuse new life into Chrysler, I think of his capacity to be very human over twenty-five years ago. I felt the same connection and a link to him then, that I feel whenever I hear his name today.

Lee Iacocca stands out as a symbol in the legends of American business. After a brilliant career at the Ford Motor Company, including his personal guidance in creating the Mustang as the vehicle of choice for young car enthusiasts, he was recruited by a shaky Chrysler organization which was tottering on the brink of bankruptcy, if not extinction. He was a leader widely regarded for his imagination and marketing prowess; in addition it was his enormous perseverance that grudgingly prompted the financial backers, the United States government, and all the doubting employees of Chrysler to finally put their confidence in one man, Lee Iacocca.

His perseverance and ability to produce fresh and innovative car concepts led to the K-Car, the re-introduction of the streamlined LeBaron convertible, and the positioning of the Chrysler New Yorker as a premier quality entry. He gambled by building the minivan Ford would not permit him do, and then bought Jeep Motors. Those moves demanded perseverance. Today, the minivan and jeep are basic mainstays of Chrysler. His willingness to put his name, face and reputation on the line as the spokesman for Chrysler in commercials, press briefings, bank and government relations, saved jobs and made millions for American investors.

The name Lee Iacocca is synonymous with creativity and driving leadership. These deserving accolades are grounded in his singular devotion to re-make the Chrysler Corporation. That devotion was manifested in his steadfast perseverance.

You have the same inherent power of perseverance within. Let it begin with one small act which inspires greater actions. Break the turbulent surface of what's not working and let your natural perseverance propel you to calmer waters. A leader takes notice of who is around him, and through actions or words, brings others into the fold.

REFLECTIONS ON
LEE IACCOCA

Characteristic of PERSEVERANCE
By: Bill Brunner, President
Brunner Motors

On November 2, 1978, Chrysler announced third quarter losses of $160 million and that Lee Iaccoca was joining the company as president: just what we needed as dealers, a manufacturer with weak products, no plans, poor quality, cash problems, and a new guy from Ford. To the public, Chrysler was going down the tubes fast. But, with Iaccoca inside, we started to see things change for the best. With "Government Loan Guarantees for

Chrysler" as the headline of the year, Iaccoca told dealers "you got . . . to believe." He persuaded us to "buy into" the vision of a new Chrysler and sell the story to anyone who would listen; it worked.

I will never forget the first time I met Lee at a cocktail party. My friend Susan, now my wife, and I watched him as he greeted hundreds of dealers. Suddenly, he was in front of us reaching out to take Susan's hand and ask how we were enjoying Las Vegas. He made us both feel incredibly welcomed in the several minutes of conversation that followed.

Iacocca's perseverance to lead, and his capacity to communicate, sometimes with charm, sometimes with tough words, are what made him second to none as a leader. Against all odds, he convinced factory, labor and dealers to work together as "Iacocca's Army," and turned Chrysler into the great company it is today.

◻ ◻ ◻

RICH RUFFALO

When sports psychologist Dr. Rob Gilbert heard I was collecting information on leaders, he suggested I seek out Rich Ruffalo. I had just finished addressing Dr. Gilbert's graduate class at Montclair State, when he told me about this extraordinary teacher, motivational speaker and athlete who had spoken to his class earlier in the semester. Though I had never heard of him, I decided to contact him.

Rich is a wonderful person, a powerfully magnetic speaker. He is also a professional athlete and a biology teacher. He's a giant of a man, who loves to throw the discus, shot-put and the javelin. He's a high achiever who will talk to you about your promise, your possibility and the attitude you need to succeed. His passion in life is his love for the children he teaches.

In 1995, he was named Teacher of the Year by the Disney and McDonald Corporations. That distinction put him on *Good Morning America,* and brought him national attention. There are plans for a movie about his life, and Rich is working on his memoirs. What makes his accomplishments all the more outstanding, is the fact that Rich Ruffalo is blind.

Gold Medalist
Seoul, South Korea
1988

Rich Ruffalo

The night I went to call on him at his home, he opened the door and warmly welcomed me in his sharp, clear voice and said, "First, you must give me a hug." We had just settled onto his open, airy porch and begun getting to know one another when his six-year-old daughter, Sara, came bustling in on the scene with her equally enthusiastic mother, Dianne, to make sure Rich and his guest were comfortable. Sara offered to sing just one song for the guest, and, after placing her rosy cheeks close to her father's rugged face, harmonized her perfectly pitched voice with her father's sweet baritone to croon a beautiful duet version of the theme song of the American Teacher Awards, "We Have Come To Teach."

Indeed, Rich Ruffalo had come to teach. When his vision began to blur in his sophomore year of college, it did not stop him from his dream of being a teacher. And, when his sight left him completely as a result of the eye disease, retinitis pigmentosa, he was not permitted to stop teaching. His offer to resign was rejected by his principal, Michael Lally, because "Mr. Ruff," as the students called him, was a superb leader in the classroom. A proctor assistant was hired to correct papers and do the chores that required sight. Rich concluded he had been chosen to be a role model and show students that when adversity strikes, life doesn't stop; it merely changes direction on the pathway to success.

When they finished their song, Rich turned to his daughter

and said, "You see Sara, we have come to teach, just like our song says."

Rich, a lifelong jock, is the image of the fit athlete. His movements are as full of grace as they are of power. He had always been a Class-A competitor in high school and college, with a specialty in the javelin. Rich only began to compete in the shot-put and discus when he was totally blind.

The loss of his sight created a huge vacuum in his life. It induced an uncharacteristic despondency in him, until he discovered the United States Association for Blind Athletes. Through them, he was introduced to the Paralympics, which brought together the premier disabled athletes of the world to compete. Newly inspired, Rich went on to win twenty national titles and set fifteen national records in track and field. In international competition, he achieved fourteen gold medals, including the 1988 Paralympic javelin record in Seoul, Korea.

It was a chance meeting on the athletic field that clarified in his mind, the reason for his blindness; it made him realize that when he lost his sight, he ultimately gained his vision.

On June 9, 1984, while competing in a St. Louis track event, a thread of life was passed to him, the way a runner is passed a baton; it ignited his leader within. Before that day, all of his competitive, athletic competitions had been focused on the objective of lifting his personal sense of worth and self-esteem. The operative words in his meets were me, myself and I.

As he prepared for his event, he felt a tug on his arm, and heard a small voice say, "Mr. Ruffalo, I am here with the children of the St. Louis School for the Blind, and they are here with me now hoping you will let them 'see' your arm and feel your strength." Bewildered at first, Rich knelt down on one knee. The blind children came up to him, one by one, to run their fingers over his well-veined hands, to rub the texture of his muscular arms and shoulders, and finally to kiss his cheek in gratitude.

On that day in St. Louis, as he set a new record in the javelin throw, and heard the special roar of excitement from the cluster of blind children, he knew that his own loss of sight was a gift to inspire him to lead others to sense their own promise in life.

Since that day, when an internal light kindled his life's purpose, he has dedicated himself to leading others to an awareness of the gold they can find within themselves, and in other people, by reaching out with kindness and inspiration to those who cross their paths.

Rich Ruffalo vibrates with enthusiasm. He is most satisfied when he is given the opportunity to provide the leadership insights of hope and possibility to whoever comes before him, be they students, aspiring athletes, teachers or business people. As an acknowledged leader who inspires others to persevere in their possibilities, Rich Ruffalo has ignited the lives of those who cross his path by igniting his leader within.

❑   ❑   ❑

❝ Like many people, I feel I am an amalgam person of humanity. Rich Ruffalo could be John or Jane Doe. I picture perseverance as walking through storms, crevasses, deep chasms, mud, muck and mire. After moving forward, falling down many times and thinking, should I get up, the persevering soul gets up. And, it is going to take a bigger blow to fell him, or her, the next time. The persevering soul keeps moving forward with vision and with focus, while locked on the dreams that lie ahead.

No matter what happens or befalls you, if your senses are locked upon that dream, and you take steps to begin to walk the mental mile toward it, the condition you are in will be forgotten instantly when you taste the sweet nectar of your victory. ❞

—Rich Ruffalo

73

PART SIX

The Power Of Passion

☐ Emotional, Psychological & Spiritual Gift

☐ Consumes Leaders In Pursuit of Objectives

☐ Feel Its Fire

Passion is a great power. Leaders have a passion that usually emerges in pursuit of an objective. It is not diligence, not simply being committed to a goal. It is a passion that consumes them in the pursuit of that objective. You can feel its fire. That passion stimulates followers who are sparked into helping leaders reach their objectives.

Too often we think of passion purely in physical terms. It is a great gift because it's also emotional, psychological and spiritual.

WAYNE HUIZENGA

Of course, a leader sees the glass half-full. A leader also sees opportunities where others do not.

The name Wayne Huizenga is revered throughout South Florida as a successful man whose leadership began not in newspapers, oil, or real estate, but in waste. A third-generation garbage man, he dropped out of college in 1962. He took a small trash removal business and turned it into a mega operation that dominated the landscape of South Florida.

From that base, Wayne Huizenga's instinct guided his attention to the small video rental operation that his innovative eye pictured as having nationwide franchise potential. It would be so big that only one name, "Blockbuster," would fit. It is now a household word. In fact, he only reluctantly agreed to consider investing in a budding movie rental business. Once he bought into the company, his passion inspired high velocity growth. In 1986 more than 1,000 stores bore the Blockbuster name, while new stores began opening every seventeen hours.

As his vision and capacity to build accelerated, Huizenga brought his touch to the Florida Marlins, a new baseball team franchise, and a host of other new businesses that created jobs, careers, opportunities and satisfaction to thousands of associates who were influenced by his innovative leadership.

When Blockbuster was sold to Viacom in 1994, for a reported eight billion dollars, Wayne Huizenga refocused his passion on launching Republic Industries with the acquisition of an Atlanta, Georgia waste hauler firm in 1995. In one year of having the laser of his leadership on that company, it had the best single performance on Wall Street in 1995, the value of its stock increasing by 964 percent.

My family's condominium in Pompano Beach, Florida includes a three time weekly trash removal system. As an early riser who heads out for a beach hike at 6:00am, I have often exchanged daybreak greetings with the trash collectors. During one of those early morning salutes, I was impressed not only by the neat, pressed uniform of the collector, but brightened by his cheerful comment, "have a wonderful day for yourself, sir!"

Three mornings later, the same sparkling truck and collector were on the grounds. I told him how impressed I was not only with his professionalism, but with those ever clean, pressed uniforms. Curious, I asked whether his truck, uniform and attitude were typical of the business.

"Oh yes," he replied. "Our customers are all treated to the best we can give them." I asked when that attitude took root in this company. He replied, "It all started with Mr. Wayne, who owned our company in an earlier day, and taught us to be customer relation specialists. Mr. Wayne went on to greater business achievement, but he left us with the gift of permanent dignity in our work."

"The Mr. Wayne" was Wayne Huizenga, who had borrowed $5,000, in 1962, to buy a Fort Lauderdale, Florida single trash removal truck with just twenty commercial accounts. With that one truck, he went on to create one of the largest waste handlers in the world, Waste Management, Inc.

Wayne Huizenga

Wayne Huizenga riveted the passion of his leadership on that business. He is described by friends as a leader who matches the sunny Florida climate with his powers of persuasion, enthusiasm and sheer exuberance. Handling garbage is tough, sweaty, grimy, work with sharp competition and customers who expect uninterrupted service. Wayne Huizenga's belief that, "The most important thing is the customer," is a tenet of his success. "No matter what it takes or what it costs, you had better do right by the customer. You keep each customer happy, and you secure your business base."

Another of his cardinal rules was cleanliness. His garbage trucks were always clean and painted; they sparkled. Employees looked sharp in neat, defining uniforms. Every employee was trained to have respect and show a positive attitude toward every client.

An early partner, Dean Buntrock, described Mr. Wayne's passion for employee excellence, "His personal drive creates an aura of excitement. He has a great sense of humor and a great sense of what motivates his employees to excel." He would always give his greatest personal gift, time, to people. Whether it was a truck driver, helper or laborer in a landfill, he always took the time to talk to people.

The ability to bring the passion of his leadership to motivate people guided Wayne Huizenga in building not just one, but two, now heading for three—billion dollar empires.

In regards to Wayne's passion and leadership, one of his closest colleagues, Steve Berrard, said, "Anyone who works with, or for, Wayne, will get a close-up of the inner standard that drives him, the striving for perfection that goes beyond the excitement of business. Wayne is always himself and makes his associates proud to be on his team."

As that smiling trash collector said, "We sparkle because Mr. Wayne showed us the way." Wayne Huizenga has consistently and generously brought the passion of his leadership to create businesses that "show the way" across America's landscape. With his latest ventures, AutoNation and CarChoice operations, Wayne Huizenga is planning to revolutionize the used car business, literally taking his "blockbuster" know-how on the road. Each major business has been different. What has been the same for each is the infusion of the passion of his leadership into everything he does.

◻ ◻ ◻

❝ I don't know about you or anyone else, but I can't sell what I don't believe in. Some guys can tell you it's the greatest used car you've ever seen, and they know it isn't, but I can't.

I can't be convincing unless I really, really believe in the product, and have the passion to see that what-

ever we're doing succeeds. I think most people are probably that way. I think passion is necessary in getting your message across, because part of conveying your message is being able to sit across the desk from a guy who you know is not just listening to what you're saying. He's looking in your eyes. He can see whether the fire is there or not. I think you really have to know what you're doing and believe in what you're doing. If you bring passion to that, then the rest is a lot easier.

I think people do have talents, including passion. While some choose to use them, for whatever reason, others do not. Maybe it's time constraints, or family constraints. Maybe they just don't have the drive or the desire. But, whatever the reason, the key issue: is do they choose to use the talents within them or do they not choose to use them? **"**

—**Wayne Huizenga**

☐ ☐ ☐

GENERAL JOHN STANFORD

General John Stanford has elevated his leader within, so that his leadership characteristics are visible for miles. He brings passion to whatever he does. Not only that, he leaves some of it behind for others to find, hold onto, and ultimately share. His passion and commitment are constant.

During a highly decorated, thirty-year Army career, he was saluted for his vital planning and leadership roles in the Gulf War. After a potently successful stint as a county executive in Georgia, the Seattle, Washington school board was drawn to his leadership, recruited him, and put the destiny of almost 50,000 school children into his hands. General Stanford never spent a day in the class-

General Stanford

room as a teacher, but as superintendent of all the schools in Seattle, he has had a tremendous impact on the lives of many youngsters. I was intrigued by this stunning accomplishment and went out west to meet him. We hit it off right away.

Over an early morning breakfast, the general answered my question about what his earliest memories were of the factors which influenced leadership.

"Mission, vision, values," he said, "these were the lessons I learned at the simple, glazed metal-top kitchen table, as I watched my mother and father teach each other to read and write. They did their lessons each night, while I learned the same skills as a first grade child."

The more the general spoke, the more vividly I felt the difficulties and triumphs of his youth. He continued, "My mom and dad taught me, by example, the meaning of their personal mission, their personal vision and their personal values, as they struggled each night to overcome their lack of even a grade school education."

He proudly added that his parents also taught him to avoid greed, avarice, hate, racism and, most importantly, to have confidence in himself. "They made me believe I could achieve anything I set my mind and God-given talents to." It seemed as if the first medals he wore proudly were the ones his parents gave him, the ones only his soul could see.

As an African-American from working class Yeardon, Pennsylvania, he attended public school. Though the only African-American in the class, he was elected class president for three consecutive years. After graduating from Penn State, and receiving his master's degree from Central Michigan University, he chose the U.S. Army as the place to hone his instinctive leadership characteristics.

After his distinguished military career, he accepted the position of county executive in Georgia. There, he found a dispirited work force reeling from the shock of scandal from the previous administration. Employees were simply going through the motions, entrapped by mediocrity. General Stanford swiftly gave the county staffers a defined mission, defined vision and defined set of values. County operations became dramatically more productive. And, attitudes soared as employees sensed their part in a dynamic operation. Ignited by the leadership of John Stanford, there was no turning back.

General Stanford brings his own childhood to all the children of the Seattle school system. So many children today, all over the country, live lives unnourished by mentors or role models. A lot of youngsters go through the school system and do not understand that they are cared for. Over breakfast, the General looked directly at me and began to talk to me about the love he brings to children. He tells them, "I'm here because I love you."

"I must leave you at 8:30am sharp," he said. "My car is waiting outside to take me directly to the helicopter that will fly me to one of the schools I'm visiting this morning. The children there have been asked to assemble in the school yard. They don't know yet, but when they are outside at 9:00am sharp, the door of that helicopter will open, and the superintendent of schools will glide down a rope into the schoolyard. That will be a memorable morning for the children! They'll remember the reason for my dramatic entrance; it is to show them that I love them. That's the first thing they need to know. And I'll tell them, I'm here because you're worthy," he added. "I'm here because you're special. I'm here because I love you."

Without a doubt, General John Stanford knows how to be an enthusiast about his work! Because of such passion, the Seattle school system now has a new rhythm, pace and pride. As reflected by General Stanford, passion is a gift we have within us; it's not something we have to learn.

❝ When asked about his view of passion as a characteristic of leadership, he paused and gazed thoughtfully. "Love is the constant," he said. "Passion ebbs and flows. The steady state is to be in love with the mission, the people and the process — and — to be passionate about those things."

"The leader," he added, "needs to understand the fire that is in people, the spark waiting to be kindled. The leader understands the principles of love, passion and leadership. In a selfless way, he fans those sparks in individuals until they become bonfires of possibilities. Passion ignites a contagious optimism."

Looking me directly in the eyes, as firm in his glance as in his erect posture, he said, "It is the passion ignited in those around me that finally fuels my own passion. I only see myself through others who are reacting to me. ❞

—**General John Stanford**

❏   ❏   ❏

ERNEST BOYER

Dr. Ernest Boyer distinguished himself as a leader in Albany, and his presence was also felt around the nation. His star sparkled as he was one of the brightest of America's premier educators and leaders, and as he served as the head of the Carnegie Foundation. Previously, he had been United States Commissioner of Education under President Jimmy Carter, and before that, Chancellor of New York's prestigious state university system. Possessed of a keen intellect, he was a man of integrity, a man of compassion and a man of passion. Everyday, he brought that passion to his work.

You could see his passion coming toward you in the same manner in which you first observed his wavy mane of striking white hair. Up close, you could see the passion and intensity that gleamed in his eyes and ignited the leader within.

Like a well-stoked, fiery engine, he kept the massive university system on the track of excellence and brought his exuberance for leadership to every activity of his life. When the major newspapers carried his obituary after he died of cancer, they noted that once, while his wife, Kay, drove him home after a chemotherapy treatment, he was conducting a conference call on the car phone.

Ernest Boyer

My first encounter with Dr. Boyer was memorable because of the circumstances which brought us together. It did not exactly have the mark of lifelong friendship written all over it. At the time, Ernie was the head of New York's State University system and was furnished with a mansion residence for official use. During the same period, the state had begun to reduce the number of its personnel. People were being fired left and right.

The *Albany Times Union* reacted to these layoffs with daily page-one profiles of individual persons who had been pink-slipped. The profiles described their salaries, mortgage payments, college tuitions, etc. Our reporters did an outstanding job in humanizing the impact of the ongoing layoffs by the state. Their daily research on state expenditures revealed the imbalance between continued unabated spending by the state, and people who were losing security, dignity and hope. It seemed the scales had been tipped unfairly.

On one of the days the *Times Union* profiled three individuals who had lost their jobs, an accompanying article described an equal amount of money that the state was spending to support the chancellor's mansion. A photo of the residence included an inset head-shot of the handsome Dr. Boyer.

That evening, I received a phone call at home from Ernest Boyer. He said that the *Times Union* article had caused him to have the most painful day of his professional life. But, that was not the entire reason he called. He quickly added that he believed the newspaper had done the right thing by exposing areas where the state could cut costs in an effort to save jobs. That call resulted in a lasting friendship that taught me that Ernest Boyer relied on and used his elegant passion as a key in exercising his leadership.

A further example of his leadership came one day when we had lunch at L'Auberge, a downtown Albany restaurant that sits on the edge of the Hudson River. He was anxious to share a university committee's recommendation to locate a new, central administration headquarters building in East Greenbush, a remote farmland east of Albany. The artist's rendering of the proposed building was a stark, all-glass, multi-story facility. It resembled an ice-cube; it was cold and without warmth.

Dr. Boyer asked for my reaction. I told him I preferred not to comment. When pressed, I finally said I felt his passion was missing from the project. It was, in my view, a barren, remote site, with a perfunctory building that looked like an insurance company office.

As we left the restaurant, I turned to my right and pointed to the abandoned former headquarters of the D & H Railroad located on Albany's eastern edge, in the shadow of the State Capital. Despite its ramshackled look and plywood covered windows, it was still a handsome gothic stone building. I remarked to Dr. Boyer that if he brought the passion of his leadership to restore the D&H building, then he would make a permanent contribution to downtown Albany's continuing renaissance.

Today, when visitors go to the headquarters of the state's university system in Albany, they do not travel to a remote suburban location and stare at an unremarkable glass building. Instead, they enter the majestic gothic building that stands as a permanent testimony to the passion of Dr. Ernest Boyer's leadership. Whenever a student begins his college experience, he'll have a silent partner by the name of Dr. Ernest Boyer.

REFLECTIONS ON

ERNEST BOYER

Characteristic of PASSION
By: President and Mrs. Clinton

"Ernie was one of the finest people we've known, not to mention one of our nation's most dedicated and influential education reformers. He was an inspiration to both of us and to countless others around the nation. He recognized early the importance of teaching, service, and learning, and he became one of our most effective advocates for reform. His legacy will live on well into the next century."

By: Former President Jimmy Carter

"He has set an example of leadership that I trust will be emulated by future generations of educators."

PART SEVEN

The Power Of Character

- [ ] Leaders Avoid Shortcuts In Ethics
- [ ] Demonstrate Value Systems In Place
- [ ] Pride Emanates From Character Of Leaders

L eaders do the right thing. They choose character. Leaders avoid the shortcuts where ethics are abbreviated. They calibrate the consequences of their actions and send that clear message to their associates. The leader provides example by continually demonstrating to his colleagues that there is a value system in place which attaches to the leader's stewardship. The value system is an absolute component of the operation. The spirit that fills the atmosphere and prompts pride emanates from the character of the leader. Leaders set the example. They cultivate commitment and inspire admiration and respect for the institutional values that are the soul of the organization.

Frank Nigro

When I returned from the Navy and resumed my job as a classified salesman, the greater revenue and personal earnings were being generated by retail advertising salesmen. My colleagues at the *Albany Times Union* and I were in direct competition with the Gannett owned *Knickerbocker News*. I went to our advertising director, Mark Collins, and proposed that I be given an opportunity to handle the retail advertising food category. The competing *Knickerbocker News* had 100% of the food advertising, because, historically, it was the city newspaper that serviced a more cohesive audience as compared to the wide area distribution of our morning newspaper.

I told Mr. Collins that if he gave me a six month trial period to manage the food category, I would also continue to handle my classified job. If he felt I was falling down on the job, he could stop the experiment. Mr. Collins gave me the opportunity, but insisted I give up the classified territory. So, I left my old job and began a new sales position with zero business.

◻ ◻ ◻

rank J. Nigro was the leading food merchant in Albany. He owned the Albany Public Markets which he literally built up from a single corner outside vegetable bin. I began to call on Frank Nigro every day with a new idea. I would take his ads from the competitive press, add a little spin, and show him how much more effective and punchy they could be. I'd bring him some piece of research each and every day.

Years later, because I had been very close to him, he told me my inventiveness and diligence had always intrigued him. In contrast with the others who were working in the business he had built, he said I always represented a fresh new promise for him. I don't believe I had the food category for sixty days when Frank Nigro astonished me by splitting his schedule. Instead of running ten pages a week exclusively in the *Knickerbocker News*, he ran five pages with each of us. Within one year, *The Times Union* owned the food category; within two years it acquired the *Knickerbocker News*.

Seeing Frank Nigro every day allowed me to view, first-hand, the integrity of his relationship with every vendor, supplier and employee. I often met him at the customer service area of his main store exactly when a customer arrived with a complaint about an item. He always acted immediately and, with great courtesy, gave the customer a replacement item or his money back. In those instances, the customer always went away satisfied.

Every employee was treated with trust. He would chat amicably with each one, underscoring the fact that his grocery empire was built on this simple credo: if you do the right thing with everyone with whom you come in contact, the majority will do the right thing for you. His character was the cornerstone of his leadership and became part of the foundation of those under his influence.

About three years into my relationship with FJN, as he was called, I applied for the new position of retail advertising manager at the newspaper, but was told I was too young. That afternoon I paid my regular visit to Frank. He took one look at me and said, "You don't seem to be yourself. What's the problem?"

I explained what had happened.

"That's not a problem. Go down and resign this afternoon."

"Frank," I said, "I have a wife and child. I can't resign."

"No, no. You resign and come to work for me. You'll become my advertising and sales promotion director for the food chain. You can also become the promotion director of the shopping center I'm opening."

Frank Nigro

So, I quit without notice and went to work for Frank Nigro. My first weekend was the inventory weekend. I went with Frank to the baby food section, and, together, we did the inventory. He said nothing the first half hour, then finally asked me, "why do you think we're doing the baby food inventory?"

"I don't know. It's such a tedious job," I answered.

"Exactly. Inventory is not interesting; inventory is a drudge. The worst inventory job in the store is the baby food. I do that job and everyone notices. The leader must always be prepared to participate, to do the right thing. In the end," he added, "the whole company's shadow is an extension of the leader's being a model for all his associates."

Within six weeks, the newspaper management called me up and asked me out to lunch. I told Frank, and he encouraged me to go. When I went, the newspaper's senior manager said, "We've been thinking this over and concluded you're really not so young. We'd like you to come back and take the job of retail advertising manager. I went back to Frank Nigro after lunch and said, "This is an awkward situation, but..."

"Don't even say anything," he replied. "They now want you to be retail advertising manager of the paper."

"Yes."

"I knew that would happen. I was only giving you a port in the storm. I only wanted to provide you with a harbor until the newspaper thought things through."

Years later, while I was giving a speech at the Albany Chamber of Commerce dinner, an envelope was handed to me while I was at the podium. The note inside read, "Please call Mr. Nigro." I finished the speech and called FJN. He asked me if I could please come over to see him. When I arrived at his warehouse office, his three sons were sitting in the reception area. "He's waiting for you inside," they said.

I went in and found Frank sitting at his desk in tears. He said, "I sold my child today."

"Frank, what do you mean?"

"Rather than leaving it to some accidental destiny, I concluded that the Albany Public Market would be better served by a larger company. Today I signed the papers." He said the new owners agreed that I could write the release. "I don't know how," he added. "I called because I thought you could help me."

I sat down in front of the typewriter at his desk and wrote the story about FJN and the sale of Albany Public Markets to Weiss

Markets before driving it over to the newspaper. It appeared in the next morning's edition. Frank J. Nigro did not go from owning a one bin vegetable stand to being the owner of the largest supermarket chain in Albany because he could effectively manage the purchase of the produce and the demonstration and marketing of lettuce and oranges. He chose to use his leadership capabilities to take his vision forward, build greatness, employ hundreds of people and always commit to doing the right thing. He could have managed a single vegetable bin for the rest of his life but his leadership ability spawned a garden of opportunity for him and for all those who crossed his path instead.

REFLECTIONS ON

FRANK NIGRO

Characteristic of CHARACTER
By: Bob Danzig

By the time we moved into our brand new newspaper plant in Albany the first year I was publisher, we had completed the construction of a magnificent suburban facility. The first day we showed up at the new building, the general manager of the newspaper met me at the door. He showed me a private parking lot next to the front door that had my name, as well as the names of all the other senior executives on specific spots.

"This is your little surprise," he said.

"I won't be parking here," I replied. "I will be parking at the most distant end of the lot. We have a lot of older people here. I'm a young publisher. When we have people trekking through *the winter ice and snow, I don't want them to get up here and see that I park next to the front door. I don't think that shows much character. Take my sign down," I said. "If the others want to park here, I will leave that decision to them. For myself, I will be parking at the very end of the parking lot."*

Perhaps that's a very modest example of character, but a very important aspect of leadership is in being sensitive to opportunities like this. To this day, when I go back to visit that paper and walk through that building, the kind of good will that comes my way, from people who were there when I was publisher, is palpable. They remember that if they had to park at the end of the parking lot, so did I.

Something tells me I probably learned that lesson by standing next to Frank Nigro counting the baby food that inventory night, when he affirmed his simple business credo to do the right thing.

By: Frank J. Nigro, Jr., Frank Nigro's Son

What I remember most about my father, in regards to his business life, is how he was able to relate to numerous employees on an individual basis. On his frequent store visits, he would often greet employees by their first name. He always inquired about their personal lives and that of their families; he was willing to lend a hand if his support could improve a situation. This sensitivity to the human condition has been an example to me in my life in how I view the importance of every human being.

❑ ❑ ❑

AARON FEUERSTEIN

A fire in a small New England mill, during the Christmas of 1995, turned the nation's attention to the relatively quiet area of Metheum & Lawrence, Massachusetts. Not many had heard of it before, unless they knew exactly where the polar fleece in their new winter jackets came from. The town's Malden Mills was a true innovator, recovering from a bankruptcy some years before when the market for fake fur collapsed, and the production of their then key product fell drastically. Through the innovation and vision of their leader, Aaron Feuerstein, they responded by becoming the industry pacesetters in polar fleece, a material that is made from recycled plastic bottles. His inspired research team was able to develop the extremely light and extremely popular fabric that was easy to dye and dry, while also satisfying ecological goals.

Aaron Feuerstein

That winter, Metheum & Lawrence were getting ready for another Christmas. Lights were strung downtown while plastic Santas and reindeer decorated the lawns and roofs of the working class neighborhoods. People had saved their money all year for the holidays when, one quiet evening, tragedy struck. The boiler exploded at the Polartec plant, destroying three of the factory's buildings, as well as the employment, security and hopes of the 2,400 employees.

Aaron Feuerstein had just completed his seventh decade. Having found ways to resist taking his manufacturing plant out of New England and out of America, he chose instead to celebrate the quality and commitment of the dedicated employees in this historic mill town. He was buoyed by the recent success in his business life and elevated in his spiritual life through his morning readings of the Talmud and his evening readings of Shakespeare.

The night that the fire blazed, the plant burned down. While the ashes were still glowing, Aaron Feuerstein called for his employees to meet him at the local Catholic high school gym.

His advisors suggested that he go offshore and have his manufacturing done in a third-world country for a fraction of what he had been paying locally. But, that was not in his master plan. He walked into the hushed gymnasium. With the weight of the tragedy sitting visibly upon him, and in front of the assembled crowd, he shook the snow from the shoulders of his coat, grasped the microphone, and told his employees that the plant would be rebuilt. More importantly, everyone would be paid for the next month with health benefits intact. The employees could be certain that the plant would again be operational with jobs, security, and dignity in place. By doing this, he created a lifeline of hope for his employees. The assembled employees were awestruck. Each individual heart was touched by the character of Aaron Feuerstein doing the right thing.

Later, in explaining his action, he said, "When people saw the devastation, they were positive that this seventy year old owner would collect the insurance and just say good-bye, but we do not operate that way. We are going to operate with whatever strength we can until we have again established Malden Mills as the leader in the industry." He continued, "My father told me of the ancient Rabbi Hillel, who advised that in a situation that is devoid of morality, try to be a man and do something worthwhile. I haven't really done anything. I don't deserve credit. Corporate America has made it so that when you behave the way I did, it's abnormal."

True leaders have that instinct. They are open to the actions that build loyalty, affection, commitment, creativity and ultimately, success. Aaron Feuerstein chose to do the right thing.

❝ **Character in a leader is absolutely essential for the long-term profitability of the enterprise. In Malden's case, our decision to rebuild in the aftermath of the fire was based on two important ethical principles.**

1) It is the corporation's responsibility to be sensitive to the human equation and to extend to all its employees, both management and blue-collar, the very same kind of loyalty that the corporation needs from its employees, if its products are to be of a superior quality to its competitors' products. The CEO must follow this principle if he is to be successful in the long-run. He must resist all unethical short-run schemes which are defeating in the long-run profitability of the shareholders.

2) The corporation has a responsibility to the community. The loyalty to the community is essential if the employees are to have a feeling of belonging, that the rug will not be pulled out from under them. In addition, CEO's who desert the community for cheap labor elsewhere, are causing the downfall of major American cities. This will eventually destroy the very prosperity which the U.S. now has, and will ultimately destroy the American system of free enterprise.

As Hillel said 2000 years ago, "not all the businessmen who accumulate fortunes are wise in God's eyes, or, in modern-day parlance, not every modern-day CEO who makes a killing with his stock options, by cutting back on employees, is truly intelligent. If you want to be wise in God's eyes, then in times of crisis, where there are no Men, where the humane-imperative is wanting, then try your best to be a Mensch. ❞

—Aaron Feuerstein

General Robert McDermott, "McD"

In more than two decades of regular business travel to San Antonio, Texas, one comes to know the rhythm of the city's charm and gentility. These vivid attributes are nourished by a cadre of activist citizen leaders who have sustained a pace of energy and aspiration to keep San Antonio's small town intimacy intact. They also keep in step with the dynamic development that makes San Antonio one of the southwest's premier tourist and business destination points.

General McDermott

Many names are regularly mentioned when the topic of leadership is on the table. One name, however, always seems to be on everyone's short list of leaders whose personal imprint impacted San Antonio's destiny. This name belongs to General Robert McDermott, also known to all as "McD."

Born in tiny Readville, Massachusetts, where he says he "learned team play since, in a little town, every woman is your mother, and every father is every child's father. If I went down the street, fell down and scraped my knee, some mother would take me in, wash it, tear a sheet and wrap a bandage around my leg, and send me home."

Young McD was inspired by the trailblazing Charles Lindbergh to attend the US Military Academy at West Point, and begin what would become a brilliant career in the Army Air Corps. After earning an MBA from Harvard University, he went on to become a command pilot, staff officer, and the first permanent dean of the U.S. Air Force Academy.

Upon military retirement, he was recruited to be the new Chief Executive Officer of USAA, a property and casualty insurance company for military officers and their dependents. His leadership instantly changed the culture of the company with his strong emphasis on technology as a tool to open new business opportunities, and new growth rose to $30 plus billion in owned and managed assets. USAA grew from being an insurance company for military officers to being the fifth largest insurer of private passenger automobiles and top ranking home insurer. It became as well, a diversified financial services firm serving people world-wide; a Fortune 500 Company.

The record of McD's achievements is vivid. What is not so immediately apparent is the fundamental leadership values that he has brought to his every endeavor. When one of the new San Antonio science facilities was dedicated to him he said, "People who work here make me look good. I try to teach them that the path to job satisfaction is to do the right thing for the right reasons; love thy neighbor as thyself. How do you express that love? Get to know yourself. Find out what your talents are. Develop your talents. Only then can you love and serve your neighbor. Only then will you find the pathway to the bottom line that really counts."

McD approached each day buttressed by the philosophy of leading with character. It was infused into the spirit of his company and paid off in attitude and productivity from all of his colleagues. A former associate, Ken Little, now editor and publisher of the "Presbyterian Survey," describes the Robert McDermott leadership this way, "For any organization, company or city to move from dead center, there has to be a leader with a vision of how things can be. It is easy to find people who can dream dreams; it's another to find people who can put them into action. I'd like to think that all the good things that have happened to San Antonio would have happened, but I think that without McD, they would not have happened as quickly, nor as positively."

All these accolades are tributes to the achievements of McD. In offering an insight into the leadership character behind his achievements, he points to a framed comic strip in his office which sums up his beliefs. In the frame is a *Dennis the Menace* strip which reads, "The best thing you can do is get very good at being you."

Reflecting on that strip, McD muses, "I am very proud to say the employees of USAA do things for the right reasons. Because our results are so good, people will listen if I speak, and recognition may flow my way because I have enjoyed that platform. However, at the root, all the activities in San Antonio, all the impressive results at USAA, and all the accolades of my military career are about the same simple truth; do the right thing."

The first "harder right" McD chose in his military career occurred in 1954 when he left the faculty at West Point to become the academic architect of the Air Force Academy. He took on nearly 150 years of tradition and culture embedded in the other older academies, by instituting new approaches to learning, as well as dramatically broadening the curriculum at the nation's fledgling academy. In the words of General John S. Pustay, Assistant Dean of the Air Force Academy, "Few are aware of the major obstacles, the tremendous investments of time, intellect and emotion that went into bringing about these changes, which ultimately were adopted by the Air Force Academy's sister institutions."

He displayed character by doing the right thing.

At the ceremony on November 30, 1989 announcing the Robert F. McDermott Chair in Academic Excellence, Under Secretary of the Air Force, Anne H. Foreman, talked about General McDermott's leadership at the Air Force Academy. "General McDermott recognized that the military academies and the military services need, in their leaders, well-rounded individuals who are not just academically talented, but are also physically and morally fit . . . General McDermott's ideas prevailed, I suspect in part because of force of personality, intellectual courage and perseverance, but also because he was right . . . not only the Air Force Academy, but also the other service academies followed his lead . . . it is clear that General McDermott deserves to take his place alongside Thayer as the Father of Modern Education."

McD's second career as President and CEO of USAA was indeed successful, and, in the end, happy because he chose the "harder right." His successes were recognized by *Fortune Magazine* in 1994, when it selected him as a Laureate in the National

Business Hall of Fame. He was also inducted by the International Insurance Society, Inc., in 1996, into the Insurance Hall of Fame.

Just as he changed the breadth and depth of the operations and offerings at USAA from insurance to a supermarket of financial services with managed assets growing 150 times over 25 years, he led his board of directors on a steep and rapid climb to fame.

With McD guidance, "The Golden Rule culture" the company embraced led to an employee commitment to self-development. At any given time, 35% of USAA employees are enrolled in college or professional courses with tuition reimbursement guaranteed. The complement to the voluntary education program is a training program that matches employee talents to job requirements.

The resulting productivity gains from these innovations give USAA the lowest expense ratio for doing business among the ten largest insurers. Besides the upward mobility gains for employees, is the commitment derived from self-development, and the "Golden Rule" that has led to employees giving time and talent to volunteer programs unmatched by any other company in the nation.

Leaders choose character. They walk the path of General Robert McDermott. They do the right thing.

Reflecting on USAA's success based on a culture of service and doing the right thing, McD offers these thoughts as the hope for mankind as we approach the millennium:

❝ *It is a matter of grave concern to me that the modern slogan for the pursuit of happiness and success has become 'knowledge is power.' It is my hope for planet earth that the leaders of the 21st century adopt the slogan 'integrity is power.' We dare not let the explosive developments of science and technology obliterate the development of character as the driving force for man's behavior.* ❞

—General Robert McDermott

GENE ROBB

Though he was not a tall man, Gene Robb was a towering figure who left a subtle, but permanent imprint on my life, like a watermark on fine paper. He didn't just touch my life, he guided me as well. A gentle man, with movie-star good looks, Gene was both a lawyer and a journalist. He was truly a refined man with an uncommon air of elegance about him. He manifested these qualities of leadership in a subdued but effective way. As publisher, he breathed his personal integrity into every aspect of the *Albany Times Union*. This personal contribution stood for something, and continues to stand for something in the Albany community today.

Gene Robb

Gene became publisher of the *Albany Times Union* when the newspaper was perilously close to failing, due to a vicious long term battle with a rival newspaper. During the years of intense competition, every line of advertising became crucial for the revenue it brought to the wobbling enterprise. That income included the legal advertising the city and county of Albany were obliged to run in a newspaper.

Albany was controlled for half a century by the O'Connell political machine, one of the oldest boss-influenced organizations in the nation. When Gene Robb arrived as publisher, he brought with him his essential core requirement for the newspaper: that it be a public advocate, the watchdog, as it were, over corruption and the abuse and illegal use of the taxpayers' money. He breathed strong character into the editorial commentary of the newspaper and unleashed investigative reporting to examine aggressively questionable "machine" manipulation of the citizens' taxes.

The "machine" lashed out and attacked Gene Robb. He was brought repeatedly before grand juries by the district attorney, who was probing false charges of misconduct by the newspaper. While no charge was ever sustained, and although the process was grueling, he refused to bend. Every one of the 972 employees of the newspaper understood the enormous personal pressure he endured. And, every employee was drawn to the character of his leadership. All were proud to be a part of his team. It was an unspoken but apparent characteristic of his to do the right thing.

Clear courageous editorials, backed by investigative reporting, brought the newspaper exposure as it spotlighted outrageous slum lord neglect of rental properties, abuses in "no-show" fictitious state jobs, and excessive lobbyist influence on the New York State legislature. Responses to every such report unleashed attacks on the newspaper and Gene Robb personally. Because he stayed on course, so did the Times Union; each corrective measure against a prior abuse confirmed the personal strength he inspired as a leader. He was brilliant, strategic, competitive and fair. His colleagues' respect for him was unparalleled and his character impeccable.

Gene Robb had a great passion for words; he loved the world of writing. That's what first brought us together. I was studying English literature at Siena College at night and had begun to publish small pieces in the college's literary journal, the Beverwyck, under the name R. Danzig. I was an honor student, thanks, in part, to my former shipmate Bob Myers. He launched my lifelong journey into literature, through private tutoring, when we were aboard ship together. By the time I arrived at Siena and caught the eye of Gene Robb, I was well prepared. During the day, I had become a high impact advertising salesman at the *Albany Times Union*. This success gave me quite a lot of visibility at the paper. At night I was a literature student.

Mr. Robb was on the Board of Trustees at Siena, and, therefore, received every publication the college printed, including the literary journal. One day, we were riding on the elevator at the paper when he turned to me and said, "I see an R. Danzig at Siena College writing for the Beverwyck. Is that someone related to you?"

I said, "No, Mr. Robb. That is I. I go to Siena College at night."

Our conversation ended there, but Gene Robb subsequently did something one might not be able to do today. He became intrigued because I was a successful young salesman who was going to college at night as an English major — a subject dear to his heart. Without my knowledge, he had my grades sent to him after every semester.

◻ ◻ ◻

When I graduated from Siena College in 1962, Mr. Robb asked me to join him for breakfast one Saturday morning. He told me that it was his intention to retire from the Publisher's position in 1974 and write editorials. It was over breakfast that I learned he had been keeping an eye on me, studying me as it were, and having my grades sent to his office.

He said, "I've concluded, at this time, that I would like *you* to be an optional candidate to succeed me someday. With that in mind, I am going to put you in a program where you'll go into the various disciplines of the newspaper. But, the deal will be, that whatever job you go into, if you can't cut it, you can't go back to the old job. You're not going to be a crown prince. You really must perform every assignment."

He was providing me an opportunity with a high performance bar requirement. This was a hallmark of the man who always put the emphasis on doing the right thing.

I was nourished by his personal counsel on how the on-going responsibility of a newspaper publisher is to be connected to the soul of the communities served by the newspaper. He nominated me for a Stanford University Fellowship in Journalism and I became one of twelve recipients.

He focused on area issues and explained the underpinnings of our newspaper's editorial position to me. Whether the issue was one of questioning New York State legislation practices, examining how to upgrade a local school or encouraging new recreational opportunities, he consistently advocated relying on one's sense of personal character to do the right thing.

When I returned to Albany from the Stanford University fellowship program, I became General Manager of a small paper which we had recently acquired in Schnectady, New York. That was in 1969.

When Gene died suddenly that August, I had not done many of the things he had in mind for me. I thought his passing prematurely was the interruption of my career program. I had turned down many opportunities to join other newspapers because of my direct fidelity to Gene, and indirect loyalty to Hearst. Now what would I do?

To my surprise, according to his wishes, I succeeded Gene Robb as publisher. At first, it was bewildering for me to walk into the office that was once his. He was such an unusual human being because he focused so intensely on the spirit and soul of the newspaper. That focus became part of my professional inheritance. He had taught me that we were more than a business institution, more than an employer of people. He taught me that a newspaper has to reflect the essence of its community. It cannot do this unless it is constantly nurtured by the person who sits in the publisher's chair. Those lessons were extraordinary gifts for him to pass on. They never left me.

My role in guiding all our Hearst newspapers to recognition for their journalism of distinction — an overriding objective of every one of the newspapers — was made possible when I was given the opportunity to step into the shadow of Gene Robb. I will end my career without ever feeling worthy enough to walk in his footsteps. However, I have been permanently privileged to have been inspired by his daily commitment to independent integrity — the invisible flag unfurled over the newspaper's masthead.

◻ ◻ ◻

REFLECTIONS ON

GENE ROBB

Characteristic of CHARACTER
By: Deborah Robb Twombly,
the youngest of his four children

*H*e did not spend lot of time with us, yet was proud of his children and considered "a family man." He wasn't always there for the lesser milestones in our lives, the soccer game, the athletics award or the play, but he was there for the big ones like graduations. He did not give advice on living our lives, but served as an indelible example of integrity, hard work and commitment to principle.

We knew that he was working to strengthen the newspaper and working to build and improve the community. We knew, because people came up to us and said, "You're Gene Robb's daughter? He's a saint. He helped . . . " We watched him be instrumental in creating the Saratoga Performing Arts Center. We watched him serve the Boys and Girls Club. We watched him fight city government corruption. We were Gene Robb's children wherever we went. By his example, all four of us learned to leave a place better than we found it, and that we can make a difference in the lives of others by how we live our own lives.

My mother called him a Don Quixote, but I knew it wasn't windmills he was tilting at. I saw him use his power as a publisher in responsible caring ways. As his children we lived in the shadow of a great man in a small city. In fact, because of his reputation and immense courage, people frequently remarked that they were surprised he wasn't taller.

To be sure, my father had sensitivity and feelings from which we also learned. At home, my father cried when he watched sad movies and laughed heartily at The Phil Silvers Show and

Candid Camera. *We had our hot nights around the dinner table arguing politics and ideas and whose turn it was to do the dishes. And, he was always modest about his accomplishments, never speaking of them at home, except to report the facts in a case against the Democratic machine or progress with the new newspaper plant. He was generous with his hard-earned money — clothes, schools, trips and presents, but his time went to the community.*

Ironically, that gift was his undoing. He cared for many things, but not enough for himself. It is not surprising that with so much heart he died of his one flaw, getting emotionally involved in so much. On August 19th, 1969 he died of his third heart attack. He was 59. At his funeral, one close friend shared many a person's thoughts saying, "He literally gave himself away."

□   □   □

GUILLERMO CRISTO

Although Guillermo Cristo was not in a position of leadership when I first met him, he still proved himself to be a shining example of character to those around him. He was one of 250 union printers at our large metropolitan newspaper, and except for his flashing billboard smile, seemed almost invisible among his colleagues. But, sometimes character needs the right lighting to be seen.

The printers' union was experiencing one of its greatest changes since the industrial revolution. Confronted with the electronic age, union officials were concerned about the dissolution of the printers' craft. Retraining was called for, but resistance to change persisted. A printer's art, after all, was his type.

Retraining to gain proficiency on the basic computer keyboard was key to modern technology competence. Most printers knew their resistance to retraining would not prevail in the long term; the union labor contract specified that their jobs could be replaced with new employees if they did not qualify for the keyboard jurisdiction the union claimed over the new process.

The battle of wills between our newspaper management and union leaders went on for six months with not one printer coming forward for retraining. The clock ticked toward an ugly confrontation which, in the end, could result in permanent job losses for the resistant printers.

Then, one day, one single printer came forward to register for the retraining, Guillermo Cristo. All eyes were on him by both peer union members and company officials. As he signed the forms for the new training class, one of his fellow members yelled out, "why are you betraying us?"

Guillermo Cristo

Guillermo turned to him, flashed his warm, signature smile and said, "It's the right thing to do."

Guillermo decided to exercise character that day. He chose to do the right thing even though he risked the enmity of those with whom he worked. Initially, he sat completely alone in the glass-walled training room with other employees staring at him as if he were a newborn. The logjam of tension had now broken and a trickle of printers signed up for the retraining. Within four months, the entire group of 250 was enthusiastically attending the classes. The printers became proud of their new skills, embraced the new technology and secured all those jobs. Guillermo Cristo made a difference in the job security and destiny of all his colleagues by exercising character. He simply did the right thing.

You have or will face similar decisions in your life. Usually your heart tells you the right thing to do. That correct choice can often result in changing the lives of the people around you. That is your leadership in action. Choose the right thing, as Guillermo Cristo did.

REFLECTIONS ON

G U I L L E R M O   C R I S T O

Characteristic of CHARACTER
By: Nicholas Cristo, Guillermo Cristo's Son

My father was one of the most dedicated and considerate fathers anyone could have. He always strived to educate himself, to do better the next time. He instilled that character in his whole family. He never purchased any so called "toys" for himself as many men do. Every extra penny he had, just as with every extra insight he had, went to his family. He always tried to do the right and correct thing, always tried to be flexible, always tried to adapt. My father looked for ways to work with change, to not resist it. He would be very proud of his extended family, they all reflect the sense of dedication and the high conviction to do the right thing that so characterized him.

❐　❐　❐

Interlude
What Will The Future Sound Like?

The very first thing you would have noticed when you walked into a newspaper building, twenty or twenty-five years ago, was a sound. Though it started in a composing room, full of massive individual linotype machines, the sound made its way into the entire building. Silence had no place to exist. There were also stereotype machines, which used flexible and printable print matrix. Hot lead was poured over them and took the impression of the type composition. The heavy pouring of the lead, and the clanks of the heavy lead plates moving on pulleys down into the press room, picked up where the sound of the massive linotype machines dropped off.

There was a noise factor to newspapers that was absolute. I grew up on it - the clack, clack of the linotype machine which could set type on the average of six lines of lead per minute. In fact, people who set six lines of type in a minute were considered "swifties" by the printers' union. They would shoot for an average of three and a half to four lines per minute.

The early computers helped to hyphenate and justify type for the first time. Slowly, the linotype machines were replaced by cold type, typewriters and other kinds of input devices that silenced the sounds of the composing room for the first time. The whoosh of hot lead from stereotype machines was quieted as the lead plates were replaced by plastic plates. Finally, the clank of lead plates was silenced in the pressroom as plastic formed the basic material for the printed page.

The sound went from the symphonic richness of Beethoven into the most subtle type of harp-like music. Technology changed. Everything became computerized. In just one generation, newspapers became independent of the requirement for craft trade manpower to produce everything that it did, and replaced it with new technological skills.

When I became publisher in Albany, we had 236 printers in the composing room. Today, about thirty-five remain. However, other kinds of work have been developed with other kinds of skills. The sound change is a manifestation of technology and so is the speed. We all accept the on-going challenge of change. And now, every single one of our newspapers has an on-line computer delivery service. Technology is now outside the walls and accessible through personal computers.

And now we have a future's task force, a group of smart, forward thinking people to brainstorm the way we may be doing business in 2010. What kind of distribution operation should we be considering? Should we have our own data-processing center or should we be part of a larger off site system? Should we have our own printing presses and plants, or should we be part of a larger collective? What kind of dreams should we have?

What will your future sound like?

❐ ❐ ❐

PART EIGHT

The Power Of Charisma

☐ Turn Up Your Personal Wattage

☐ Bring A Twinkle To The Eye

☐ A Little Goes A Long Way

C ertain people walk into the room and you're pulled in their direction. Even before that person speaks a word, you know you're in special company. You feel the charisma.

Charisma helps to turn up the wattage of your own leadership potential. Charisma brings a twinkle to the eye and a spring to the gait — qualities that characterize the human spirit. Charisma ensures that the message, as well as the messenger, are long remembered. For a leader, a little charisma goes a long, long way . . .

KATHARINE GRAHAM

On October 13, 1991, all of our editors and publishers went to Washington for a weekend conference. The head of our Washington bureau asked Kay Graham, the Chairman of the Washington Post Company, if she would have a conversation with our folks.

She was reluctant to do so, but, out of respect for our bureau head, she finally agreed.

That night I asked Chuck Lewis, our Washington bureau chief, to wait outside and welcome her so she wouldn't have to navigate her own way through the hotel to our meeting room. When she pulled up in her black Mercedes, Chuck went to the car to open her door. When he did so, the first thing he heard was "Shhh." A minute later a hand came out and beckoned him into the car. He put his head inside the car. Her built-in black and white television set was focused in on the Anita Hill hearings. She was riveted and said, "We'll have to wait for a break before I'll come inside."

So, there they stood in the driveway, until she was satisfied that she'd be able to leave the hearings. When she was finally introduced, her comments could not have been more cogent. The entire room full of sophisticated editors and publishers was struck by her overwhelming magnetism. She did not just say "welcome to Washington." She spoke about commitment to our industry and how it had to reside in the people who were in the room that day. If the commitment is not there, then we betray the journalistic purpose of our institutions no matter the size. She said, with all the complexities and pressures of the newspaper business, it was vital that we keep our eye on the fundamental integrity that is so much a part of our nation's history, and will always be a key to our future.

Katharine Graham

Within a few brief minutes, she spoke so elegantly, and with such charisma, that her comments galvanized us. Every newspaper professional who saw Katharine Graham knew what an extraordinary and accomplished person she was.

Upon her husband's death, she found herself a single mother, being suddenly thrust into the role of publisher of one of the great newspapers of America. In those days, however, it was a financially weak institution. She had to learn the necessary savvy to make the *Post* the business it is today.

At the time the profound, and what was acknowledged to be daring, positions she took on the publication of the Pentagon papers and Watergate were mainly looked at for their courage. While those absolutes influenced the destiny of the nation, an equally important characteristic she had, charisma, stood shoulder to shoulder with her courage.

REFLECTIONS ON

K A T H A R I N E   G R A H A M

Characteristic of CHARISMA
By: Don Graham, Katharine's Son

*W*henever I think of Katharine Graham's business career, I start at the beginning. My sister Lally and I were the "audience" for my mother's first business speech.

It was December, 1963. My father, Phil Graham, the publisher of The Washington Post since 1946, had died suddenly and tragically in August. My mother had never worked in the business side of a newspaper, unless you counted a few weeks taking circulation complaints more than 20 years earlier. After my father's death, she made a fast, but difficult, choice at the urging of the top executives at The Post Co.; she would step in as publisher of the newspaper and try to run the company.

To say that this was challenging for her, is a breathtaking understatement. The friends she and my dad had seen night after night included many reporters and editors. Journalism *and public issues had been discussed daily around the dinner table, but management, rarely.*

She was more frightened than I have ever seen her, before or since. The conventional wisdom in 1963 frowned on the idea that a woman could run a major business. My mother (she would now regret to tell you) did not wholly disagree with the conventional wisdom. Over the following 28 years, she would completely disprove it.

One of the things that frightened her most was public speaking. And, her first audience was a friendly one, The Post's employee Christmas party. As always, Mrs. Graham prepared well. She got Art Buchwald to write her speech. Lyndon Johnson had just fired the French chef who had cooked for the Kennedy White House. Mrs. Graham was to "announce" that she had hired him for The Post cafeteria.

As she practiced the speech in front of me and my sister, my mother, the chairman and publisher, later referred to as "the most powerful woman in the world," was so nervous that as she read Art's lines, her voice broke repeatedly.

Kay Graham became more confident as the year's passed, never wholly so. Oddly, the self-doubt she started with, and never completely outgrew, always seemed a key part of what made her succeed. She never fell prey to the self-certainty that afflicts so many successful people. Too far to travel.

❏ ❏ ❏

CRAIG KIELBURGER

Perhaps the phrase, "it takes a village," can also be expressed as, "it takes a child." Just one.

60 Minutes was doing a feature on the United Nations Commission for the Human Rights of Children. It caught my attention because our second daughter, Marsha, had spent the previous summer in Geneva, Switzerland, working with that same agency. The

T.V. magazine piece featured Craig Kielburger, a thirteen-year-old Canadian, who had toured Asia for seven weeks examining, confirming and publicizing the ugliness of child slave labor. His itinerary had him met at every pre-arranged point and chaperoned by local human rights advocates.

The previous year, Craig was moved by a newspaper story he had read about a boy his age in Pakistan, Iqbal Masih - whose labor, at the age of four, was traded by his family in exchange for a small loan. Iqbal spent the next six years chained to a rug loom, until he escaped and joined a crusade against child labor. Iqbal won worldwide attention, but was senselessly murdered in the streets of his village.

Craig did more than read about Iqbal, he became determined to act. He went to his own school classmates and told them about the very real problem of children like themselves, in slave labor, who were stripped of

Craig Kielburger

their childhoods. From those direct dialogues, Craig brought his natural leadership to create a group called Free the Children. He began to speak at other schools and soon had created an organization that rapidly grew in members, enthusiasm and impact. He also caught the eye of the media.

His parents, Theresa and Fred Kielburger, both teachers, reluctantly agreed to allow Craig to visit Asia in order to speak directly to the children of bondage. The trip included a moving and memorable stop at the grave of Iqbal, who had originally inspired him. The media found the story compelling and were attentive to this charismatic young leader.

During the same period, Canadian Prime Minister Jean Chretien arrived in the same area of Asia, accompanied by three hundred business leaders eager to sign several billion dollars worth of export-import deals. Craig attempted to meet with the Prime Minister to talk about the plight of children who made some of those exports. When the prime minister refused to see him, Craig held a press conference instead. The meeting with the press dominated the evening's television news back in Canada. Suddenly, the issue of child labor was catapulted onto the national agenda. The prime minister finally did meet with Craig, and gained new personal insight into the issue. Free the Children had a national standing and the work of the child volunteers gained new velocity and impact.

◻ ◻ ◻

Craig continued to bring the force of his leadership to encourage a broader public empathy for the issue of child labor. His national celebrity resulted in his being offered an advisory position in the government. Craig declined, saying he did not want to compromise the independence of Free The Children. He said that youth must retain their own vision.

In a powerful commentary on his own core principles, Craig said, "I believe that young people can make a difference, and, when speaking out, do have a lot of power. One of the best things about being young is we still have our imagination. We still think we can fly; we still think we can go to the moon. There are so many things in which you think you are unstoppable."

With a backpack full of slides illustrating the tragedy of so many children in Asia, Craig goes to forum after forum showing what he has learned and urging more privileged children to think beyond themselves. He spoke to a U.S. Congressional committee and prompted Senator Tom Harkin of Iowa to sponsor legislation which banned the importation of goods made with child labor.

Thirteen years of age, with a leadership record of inspiring accomplishment that will last for countless lifetimes, Craig Kielburger has used his charismatic personality selflessly. Exploited children have a much needed ally. He has flexed the muscle of his natural leadership. Anyone who has crossed his youthful path can envision how effective Craig will be when he fulfills his other boyhood dream to become a physician and work for the international organization, Doctors Without Borders.

Leaders do expand borders. They let their charisma flow to be a source of enrichment and encouragement. And yes, leaders do come in all sizes — and ages.

❏   ❏   ❏

❝ I believe that inspiration is a critical component of leadership. Iqbal Masih was a leader to me, because he inspired me to think beyond myself and to take action for a cause. He inspired many other boys and girls to stand up and be counted, to demand their right to be protected from exploitation, to demand their right to go to school.

I believe that a leader is someone who has a vision, who is able to communicate that vision to others and inspire them to act upon that vision. I try to inspire others to become involved in helping children by telling them stories of the children I meet, by giving the issue of child labor and the exploitation of children a human face. I do this by sharing my experiences meeting poor or exploited children who work in slave-like conditions, or who live on the streets of the world's biggest cities.

But, I am not inspiring others alone. I am inspiring others by sharing the lives, the reality, the courage and the hope of children by being their voice.

I have read that in World War I, young soldiers, inspired by their commanders, threw themselves into the line of fire of deadly machine guns. Imagine if politicians were able to inspire young people not to take up arms, but to help other people, to care for others, to protect the environment, and to take a stand *to participate in making the world a better place. Young people are waiting for leaders who have more than their own interest at heart.*

People say that I am a leader. I want to say that I have seen, in the eyes of the children who live and work in the streets of Bombay and Rio de Janeiro, real leadership. For these children, leadership means survival. Leadership means having food in your mouth at the end of the day, so you can get through the night. Leadership means negotiating with drug dealers, pimps or policemen so that you will not be hit or raped. Leadership means finding shelter for your friends when it rains or when it is cold.

I believe that a leader helps change the lives of people by giving them hope, by inspiring them, by showing them that despite the insecurities, the poverty or the problems they see, that all is not lost; things can be bettered through the effort of each one of us. 🙶

—**Craig Kielburger**

BEVERLY SILLS

One can easily look at a piano as a metaphor for life. It's made up of high as well as low notes, flats as well as sharps, ivory keys as promising as daylight and keys as dark as midnight. But, only when you put it all together can you have anything that can be called music.

One singer who has always stood out in my opinion as an example of the art form at its highest and of a life lived to its richest, most rewarding fruition, is Beverly Sills. Like a musical score dotted with whole-notes, half-notes and everything in-between, her life is marked by brilliant success, extraordinary difficulties and steadfast triumph.

In the spring of 1973, my wife, Pat, agreed to chair a fund-raiser for the Lake George Opera Company, starring Beverly Sills, the American born-and-bred diva who helped to generate interest in opera and who had performed to standing ovations and curtain-calls worldwide. Pat, diligent and committed to all things to which she turns her attention, worked for six months to make sure every single one of the 3,000 seats at the Palace Theater in Albany was sold. The spring evening was the perfect backdrop to a magnificent concert. Beverly Sills, elegant in her black evening gown, filled the stage with her singing and her outgoing presence.

Beverly Sills

When she exited, after the last ovation, the audience remained in their seats for several minutes, unwilling to move.

Following the concert, we hosted a dinner at Albany's historic Fort Orange Club. Beverly arrived with her mother, Mrs. Silverman, her husband, Peter Greenough, and their lovely daughter, Muffy. I began talking about the newspaper business with Peter, whose family had been early owners of the *Cleveland Plain Dealer* until it was sold to the Newhouse organization. At that time, Peter was writing an economics column for the *Boston Globe*. He was charming, natural, and at home with another newspaper man.

As our guests settled at the round table, we noticed for the first time that Muffy communicated with her family by sign language. Born deaf, she could only see and feel, but never hear her mother's gifted voice. Muffy handled the entire evening with grace and humor. Pat and I were enormously uplifted, not only by the concert, but by the entire Greenough family, including Mrs. Silverman, who encouraged her daughter's singing when Beverly was only a few years old.

Twenty-three years later, in May, 1996, I was thrilled to be included at a black-tie dinner and tribute to Harvey Golub, the

Chairman of American Express, at New York's Lincoln Center. The entertainment was an evening of listening to Luciano Pavarotti. The hostess that night was the now managing director of the Lincoln Center, Beverly Sills. By 5:30, word arrived that a sore throat would prevent Pavarotti from singing. The disappointed audience slumped in unison.

Immediately following dinner, the Lincoln Center's director, Beverly Sills, marched to the microphone and said with a huge smile, "How would you like to be in my shoes?" It was just the right tone and tenor (so to speak) to dissolve the evening's disappointment. She enthusiastically told us about the substitute tenor, personally recommended by Pavarotti, and then gracefully saluted Mr. Golub for the leadership he brought to Lincoln Center. The evening was defined by her charisma.

The charisma exuded that night made one of its first appearances when she was just four years old. Nicknamed "Bubbles," she had memorized the twenty-two arias on her mother's Galli-Curci recordings. She could even hit all the high notes. Inspired by her teacher, Estelle Liebling, Beverly was a natural performer who was totally at home on the stage. The girl from Brooklyn, in the borough of Kings, went on to make history by portraying some of the most famous operatic queens.

She gained a new joy when she met and married Peter Greenough. She describes herself as "smitten" when they met, while he felt he had been hit by "a thunderbolt." Her life was tested with her daughter's hearing challenge and her son's autism and institutionalization. Her answer to those challenges was to use her talents as national chairman of the Mother's March on Birth Defects.

Although she found the going difficult as she traveled the nation meeting with groups of parents of handicapped children, she discovered a power within her to bring a measure of comfort to the families of the disabled. In her autobiography, she describes the pride and gratification she experienced in raising more than fifty million dollars. It was, she said, as "satisfying as anything I have done in my operatic career."

When Harvard gave her an honorary degree, the citation read, "Her joyous personality, glorious voice and deep knowledge of music and drama bring delight to her audiences and distinction to her art."

Her impressive leadership became her strength, as she grappled with the overwhelming financial challenges of the New York City Opera, when she became director of the struggling company. A New York newspaper headline trumpeted her comment about the opera company challenges; "I won't be defeated." Beverly Sills' indomitable spirit is infusing new life into the New York City Opera." Indeed, by 1983, the attendance reached 86% of capacity and the critics heaped praise on the company's works. All this was made possible by the exercise of her charismatic leadership.

She has now reigned successfully as the senior executive responsible for the entire Lincoln Center facility in New York City. Her charismatic leadership has infused every inch of the glass, stone, fountains, musicians and voices of that great institution. Each is elevated, enriched, and inspired by the high "C" of Beverly Sill's charisma.

❑ ❑ ❑

❝ My mother used to tell me that I could do anything I wanted to do and be anything I wanted to be if I was willing to work hard enough. It was my mother who had all the charisma. She gave me the dream and I made the most of it. ❞

—Beverly Sills

Interlude

What I Learned From The Dance

Dance has been called a dialogue without words between dancer and audience. Choreographer Alvin Ailey remarked that a dance performance should entertain as well as educate. How does this relate to our concepts of work and leadership?

You do not, of course, go to work (in fact, spend one-third of your life, probably more in an office), to be entertained. In business, or in any other institution, communication must be done with words, but a distinction that separates leaders from followers is the ability to have more than one dialogue going at once. A business dialogue between those who lead and those who follow will, for the most part, get the job done. Notice that I say for the most part. For there is also an almost unspoken dialogue, with characteristics abound in energy, enthusiasm, and inspiration. Both forms of conversation need to be concurrent. A true leader knows both the spoken and the unspoken languages.

Two stories which I learned about master choreographer George Balanchine should be related here. The first was told during an interview by one of his dancers. It's a simple tale. Balanchine liked to pick out perfumes for each of his ballerinas. He knew them so well, knew who they were intrinsically and instinctively, that he was able to match dancer with scent.

As I thought about what he had done, I realized that perfume, as part of a dancer's costume, is irrelevant. No matter how close you sit to the stage, the scent will not travel. I assume that it was done purely to enhance the dancer's sense of herself — a dialogue without words between choreographer and the dancer who brings his vision to life. It was a pretty savvy move on his part as well, because without asking any questions, he knew which dancers were in the studios practicing that day.

The other story concerns his "Serenade," which he choreo-graphed in 1934, over sixty years ago. It was a ballet for the students of the School of American Ballet, set to Tchaikovsky's score. In Balanchine's own words, "one day, when all the girls rushed off the floor area we were using as a stage, one of the girls fell and began to cry. I told the pianist to keep on playing and left that bit in the dance. Another day, one of the girls was late for class, so I left that in too."

The first is a deceptively simple story of knowing someone so well, someone who executes your vision, who moves to your steps, that you are able to match her personality with a particular gift or enhancer — in this case a bottle of perfume.

The second has further implications for leadership as well. A leader, in this case, a choreographer, a genius really, witnessed unexpected moments in his choreography during a rehearsal one day. On this particular day, he decided to leave in the "errors," in much the same way a Navajo prayer rug has a deliberate flaw sewn in the weave. It wouldn't appear at first as if he had two choices, but he did. He acknowledged the unexpected, incorporated it into his work and finished the ballet. He was a true leader in every sense of the word.

There is something to be said about leaders and choreographers. Each has a particular vision that, to be brought to life, must be realized through other people. Some choreographers get an idea for a dance when they hear a piece of music that inspires in them a visualization — an interpretation as it were. Some begin with a movement and then seek out music to match their steps. The choreographer will then assign each dancer a role based on his or her particular strengths, while at the same time trying to bring out something new in each person. Of course, you give your best jumper the highest leaps and your most lithe dancer a role which conveys that physicality. But, sometimes you give a dancer the opposite of what he or she is known for, because many things can be learned from contraries or opposites. The great Irish poet William Butler Yeats wrote, "You cannot separate the dancer from the dance." Likewise, you cannot separate leadership from the leader.

Martha Graham said that it takes ten years to make a dancer. That's a lot of sweat, tears and sprains not just to the body, but to the ego as well. How long does it take to become a leader? It's hard to come up with a definite answer like Graham's, because unlike physical prowess, leadership skills are inherent. There is a spiritual component to leadership which can be enhanced through the practice of learned techniques. Basically, if the seeds of leadership are not planted within, and then nourished and fed, then those traits may lay dormant forever. Can a leader emerge later in life? Of course, but the gift is truly maximized when it is encouraged to flow regardless of age.

❏   ❏   ❏

PART NINE

The Power Of Energy & Enthusiasm

□ Spark The Engine Of Momentum

□ Elevate Your Spirit

□ Lift Your Colleagues To Higher Levels

L eaders have a natural spring to their step. Heads turn when they walk into the room. They convey a message before saying a word. They exude an energy that is palpable and forceful. That energy and enthusiasm is a natural state of mind for the leader, it sparks the engine of momentum and sets the pace.

You have energy and enthusiasm within you. You own them as basic powers of the human state. Get in touch with those values now and reflect on those circumstances that heightened your energy and enthusiasm. Like a pilot, let your natural energy and enthusiasm elevate your spirit and lift you and your colleagues to your maximum performance altitude.

HERB KELLEHER

Because so many of our newspaper properties are located in Texas, I often fly there on Southwest Airlines. Some time ago, I began to notice that when I either entered or exited the airplane,

Herb Kelleher

the jetways I walked through were filled with family pictures of the employees of Southwest Airlines. They were poster boards that cumulatively left you with the sense of a collective spirit and a collective vision. I began to think that these manifestations of pride, inclusion and plain old joy, started with one person. I became an observer of Southwest Airlines and, consequently, of the leadership of their CEO, Herb Kelleher.

I've never experienced a bad moment with Southwest that contradicts my impression. I have always been aware of the wonderful spirit of enthusiasm that permeates the airline and its employees. I'm now persuaded that spirit can be found in the personality, zest and enthusiasm of Herb Kelleher. One can hear his echo through his people.

I have often asked myself — what if I were an unsighted person, without access to those abundant family photos, would I still detect that special spirit? I concluded that the extraordinary courtesy, the bubbling enthusiasm of Southwest's people, the sense one has of being a special patron by virtue of the conduct of the pilots and flight attendants, would still have been apparent to me. I would have still been able to feel, if not see, that special spirit.

Herb Kelleher is a New Jersey native who once practiced law and who has been piloting Southwest Airlines since 1981. The airline was given little chance for survival when it had its upstart launching. Now it flies in and out of twenty four states and a large variety of cities, with planes that boast an industry high occupancy rate. Although Southwest has the identical basic assets of every other airline — planes, pilots, flight attendants, mechanics, routes and seats to fill — the company also has the energy and enthusiasm of Herb Kelleher's leadership.

Southwest regularly wins the Department of Transportation's coveted "Triple Crown" for premier customer service, on-time flights, and superior baggage handling. In 1994, the year that *Fortune* magazine named Kelleher America's best CEO, 125,000 people applied for 3,000 Southwest jobs. Perhaps that's because the CEO ascribes the airline's success to his employees, whom he describes as "Intangibles." He says straight out that he cherishes and respects his 23,000 colleagues and approaches them with the same values of humor, independence, and respect that existed the day the airline first filled a plane.

Herb says he is a zealot about Southwest Airlines' human assets who inspire customer service and quality commitment. High energy and committed employees provide a sustainable, competitive advantage in the marketplace. Herb hires employees who are open to energy and enthusiasm because they have great attitudes. He describes people with great attitudes as those who want to improve, treat others with respect, and like to laugh, especially at themselves.

Herb Kelleher has all the attributes a CEO requires to lead a successful major, complex, competitive business. What differentiates his leadership is the tidal force of energy and enthusiasm he brings to the entire Southwest family. He describes his most effective tool in maintaining that spirit as the Culture Committee which Southwest's Executive Vice President initiated. There, one hundred and seven colleagues drawn from every area, pilots to clerks, are immersed in understanding the vital spirit of Southwest. It's one thing to fly, it's another to soar. Each member of the committee is told that he or she has been chosen because of personality and dedication. They are not only employees and colleagues, they are ambassadors of Southwest.

He looks for, in his own words, a "patina of spirituality" to be the fundamental cornerstone of Southwest Airlines. That's powerful. When I walk on or off a Southwest plane and see the jetway full of the family photos of the people of Southwest Airlines, to me that's a landscape, a portrait of that special "patina of spirituality."

The leadership characteristics of Herb Kelleher make for a long parade. But, the head of his own jubilant celebration is clearly the marching band of energy and enthusiasm he brings to everyone, every day.

REFLECTIONS ON

H E R B   K E L L E H E R

Characteristic of ENERGY & ENTHUSIASM
By: Jonathan T. Shubert, Southwest Airlines Co.
Executive Communications Manager

Top Ten List of "Herb's Greatest Hits" showcase him as the Man of Action he most assuredly is. Drum roll, please:

10. He actively listens to, interacts among, and dialogues with our employees, customers, and stockholders.

9. He sets an irreverent, zany tone by maintaining and promoting a healthy sense of humor — and he welcomes reciprocated irreverence!

8. He empowers employees to grasp each and every opportunity to grow, learn and develop.

7. He emphasizes teamwork, creativity and initiative.

6. He eschews the hierarchical style organization that confuses power with responsibility, rules with management, and titles with worth. He embraces a personalized, individualized approach to leadership.

5. He takes his job and the competition seriously, but certainly not himself!

4. He sets a good example by working "days in the field" alongside ticket agents (processing tickets), baggage handlers (throwing bags) and flight attendants (guffawing with our customers).

3. He encourages employees to have fun on the job, it's mentally stimulating, spiritually liberating and makes them <u>want</u> to come to work.

2. He genuinely loves people and inexhaustibly displays sincere compassion, concern and care.

. . . and the NUMBER ONE reason Herb Kelleher is a true Man of Action:

1. He passes out PEANUTS with class and style!

◻ ◻ ◻

BILLY J. (RED) McCOMBS

Red McCombs is a unique figure within the city of San Antonio's high impact businessmen and civic leaders. Red is also a giant of a man, whose every gesture is made with finesse and grace. But, not so long ago, he was selling used cars. In fact, he had only planned to sell cars for just a few weeks. Three decades and a billion dollars in annual sales later, McCombs Enterprises is the sixth largest automobile dealer in the nation.

He has brought the same energy and enthusiasm for selling cars to his other successful interests. He has owned and sold both the Denver Nuggets and the San Antonio Spurs, and a variety of businesses including radio and television stations, ranches, oil ventures, restaurants, ski resorts and convenience stores. In his community, his diverse interests range from major medical centers to the zoo.

There is a largeness of spirit to Red McCombs that is equal to the largeness of his business frame, the largeness of his competency and the largeness of his civic leadership.

Red was my dinner companion at San Antonio's Argyle Club. When our meal was served, Red removed the top of the pepper shaker and covered his plate with a snowfall of the tiny black specks. As his plate was smothered in black, he turned to me and remarked how much he loved the spice of the pepper, just as he loved the spice of each day's opportunity to give more to the life one leads.

I've never seen a pepper shaker since without thinking of Red McCombs, not for the fact that he covered his plate with pepper, but that he chooses to bring that spice to everything which he touches.

Colleagues would quickly acknowledge Red to be big league. Buoyant. Crafty and keen. Fair and pragmatic. His leadership causes him to fill a room. He is described as being balanced beautifully between a life of public service and worthy organizations.

Energy and enthusiasm pulse from Red McCombs like a skipping stone on a calm lake surface. He is an opportunity stimulator, creating hundreds of jobs and careers for folks who have been embraced by his effervescing energy and enthusiasm. Red builds possibilities. Red creates new engines of commerce and Red has spent his entire business life turbocharged by enthusiasm and energy. He has nourished these characteristics to be paramount in his leadership.

Red McCombs

There is a Red McCombs by some other name in every city, village and town across America, who peppers his home town with the spice of what he can bring to it.

A leader may take a vacation for a little R&R, but while on the job, the day is infused with a good dose of energy and enthusiasm.

" *Every human being has energy and enthusiasm; in my mind the issue is, at what level. I am convinced that both are related more to attitude than to anything else; i.e., health, success, failure, opportunity, etc. I have believed, since I was a young boy, that every day is a gift from God that I have neither earned nor deserved. Since it is a gift that I am allowed to utilize in any of the millions of ways that I choose, it has always been very natural to me to say my attitude will create my energy and enthusiasm, I want to be certain that this energy and enthusiasm creates positive results every single day of my life.*

This outlook has never been a burden. In fact, every day is something that I look forward to. Is it easy to maintain the right kind of attitude in order to have a high level of energy and enthusiasm when the world around you has suddenly turned dark and the mountains appear so high they are impossible to climb? In my mind, it is even easier under the bleakest of circumstances than it is under the best of circumstances. The reason being that under the best of circumstances, even with high levels of energy and enthusiasm, I am more apt to lose focus than I am under dark and bleak circumstances.

Even with this outlook, from the time I was a teenager and life's realities were becoming vivid, I have never bought into the common leadership notion that "you can be anything that you want to be." I wanted to be the world's greatest athlete and the world's greatest cowboy. I didn't have the ability to do either, but I did learn through energy and enthusiasm everyone can always do better. My entire life, personal and business, is driven everyday by energy and enthusiasm that come with this attitude. **"**

—Red McCombs

IRWIN NOVAL

Next time you're walking on Park Avenue, or any large street that signifies quality commerce, take a moment and look up. You'll see countless office buildings and thousands of windows that frame offices. Imagine for a moment the lives behind the glass, so that the windows open for you like the small windows on an advent calendar. There are such stories everywhere waiting to be revealed.

Irwin Noval

One such Park Avenue window (and story) belongs to my friend, Irwin Noval. The view outside his office may be commanding, but inside, it is his presence that is even more mesmerizing. The Remington sculptures signify success.

Irwin planned to become a doctor, but at the age of eighteen, his father died suddenly. He left school when he was a pre-med college sophomore and returned home to run the family's small Brooklyn-based exterminating business. The office was in the bedroom of his mother's home, and consisted of a box of index cards and a black rotary telephone. "I didn't even know what a cockroach looked like," Irwin said. But three days after his father died, he got a call from one of the company's biggest customers who had a problem that needed solving. There were no employees to call on. So, without any prior experience, Irwin went out, "with tears in his eyes," to a baking company in Manhattan. If he saw one of the bosses coming towards him, he'd go the other way, to avoid answering any difficult questions.

Gradually, from a client base of thirty index cards, Irwin Noval built the business into the largest independent exterminating company in New York. He moved the office out of the house, first to

Bedford-Stuyvesant, and then to a few other sites before arriving on Park Avenue. His client list includes the most exclusive hotels and restaurants in Manhattan, and his company works around the clock.

Irwin's company specializes in pest control for the hotel and restaurant industry in Manhattan. In the early 80's, due to the freedom of information act, results of Board of Health inspections of restaurants became public knowledge and were published in the food columns of local newspapers.

A report of failure created in the mind's eye of the public, a vision of a filthy infested place which, in turn could cause real and substantial damage to that business. Reputations were tarnished and highly paid executives lost jobs over this issue.

If places that were unclean were the only ones affected, it would not have been so bad. The way it worked out, however, was that, too often, code enforcement was so rigid that basically clean, well-maintained places would fail for the slightest infraction. The limited presence of flies or even two roaches could cause failure the same as if there were hundreds of flies or roaches. In the beginning this kind of extreme enforcement was due to bureaucratic insensitivity. Later on, the enormous damage that the consequent publicity could inflict created opportunities for extortion. The slightest infractions were seized upon for that reason.

For many years, the restaurant industry suffered what can only be described as a reign of terror. Tremendous pressure was put on pest control companies serving food establishments to get them to "pass" inspection, including pressure to act as a conduit for bribes.

With most of his company's revenue derived from the food industry, and payoffs not an option, Irwin's company's survival was threatened. The task was daunting and the playing field not level; the stakes were a lifetime's work. Unless the problem was attacked with energy and enthusiasm, the outcome could be disastrous. As Irwin tells it, "I don't know what impels people to meet challenges like this with energy and enthusiasm. I am not sure I really know why I did. I think for me it was/is an inability to accept failure and an optimism that I have made part of my very being."

He was fortunate to work with a team of technicians, supervisors and key management people who responded to his enthusi-

133

asm and then generated their own. Meetings were held in the evening after they worked the entire day. Accounts in jeopardy were reviewed and action plans developed. Sometimes he would send a crew of men in at night to go through every inch of a hotel kitchen, with food service areas the size of a city block, in an effort to insure that an inspector would not find even one roach or fly in the entire place. Other times, when a restaurant was due for a "re-inspection," which could come at any time during a six week period, he would send a technician at six a.m., every morning until the inspection was made, to make sure everything was perfect, and that absolutely no excuse would be found to fail it.

Eventually, the corruption was uncovered, a scandal ensued, the situation was remedied and the period ended. All those years of hard work made his firm a service powerhouse with a reputation for honest, outstanding loyal service and a mountain of goodwill. In the same ensuing years, his company grew to the point where it dominated the field of pest control for New York's better hotels and restaurants.

I n the early 70's, his company served a small number of stores for one major supermarket chain in the N.Y. Metro area. At that time, prices and expected results for pest control to the supermarket industry were modest. Nevertheless, the amount of potential business, and the feeling he had that supermarkets would eventually need better quality service, attracted him to try to develop that niche.

The supermarket industry works on small profit margins. To gain market share, his prices had to be competitive and service had to be visibly better than others'. Compounding the difficulty in getting good results, especially in supermarkets, depended on many things not under his control, such as sanitation, storage practices, etc. For years his company's failures outnumbered successes. For more than a decade, however, they faced up to every failure with energy and enthusiasm taking each failure as an opportunity to improve. By viewing each negative with optimism, they improved to the point where they now service more supermarkets in the metro area than any competitors.

Irwin went to college at night, and to meet him today, you would think he had, indeed, become a doctor. He subscribes to medical journals and never lost his interest in medicine. But instead of obtaining his original dream, this man of unbounding energy turned his early misfortune and loss inside-out and created a hugely successful business.

"I have fun," Irwin gleefully remarks, "I get a bang out of life. I worked on that by growing, by becoming aware of the potential for enjoyment and by becoming involved. That means doing my best and getting satisfaction out of it. I don't think that happened by chance."

Zeal is his constant companion. Irwin is always looking for new business opportunities. We attend lectures at the 92nd Street Y on subjects such as economics, politics, and the arts. He's fascinated by scientific discoveries and "what my fellow man can accomplish." And, he's always there for each of his four children. Without a doubt, he has a voracious appetite for life.

❒ ❒ ❒

ᴸᴸ To be a leader, you inspire people to follow you and take a certain course. You cause others to act. You need inner strength and self-confidence and, of course, you have to be enthusiastic. You have to be humble, because you work with other people. It won't work if you're controlling and don't give them a chance to flower.

There's a dynamic between what you're born with, what life gives you, and what you do with it. I think everyone has the capacity to create themselves within the limits of what God gave us. One way or another, we can do an awful lot.

I worked very hard to become what I am today. Not only as a businessman, but as a person. I don't

know if I started out enthusiastic, but I became that way.

Roger Bannister ran the first four minute mile. As soon as people see what can be done, it unleashes a tremendous energy. Now look at how many people can run the four minute mile. I don't think the training was the difference, it took somebody breaking new ground. That's an exciting part of life. 🙎

—**Irwin Noval**

◻ ◻ ◻

DAVID YUNICH

David Yunich was a summer solicitor for the *Albany Times Union*. That's how I first remember the folklore surrounding the Yunich name; selling summer subscriptions door-to-door. He sold subscriptions all the way through high school and Union College, where he had a partial baseball scholarship. He was a record-breaking young salesman, engaging prospective new customers on his "cold calls." No one ever sold more subscriptions for our newspaper during the summer. He was a true legend.

He went to work at Macy's after graduating from the Harvard Business School. He was named Senior Vice President for Merchandising when he was twenty seven. He became President of Bambergers, then America's fourth largest department store, when he turned thirty four - the youngest CEO of a major company in the country. He was also one of the founders of the Young Presidents Organization.

When I first met him, he was being honored at a "State Dinner" given by the Albany Chamber of Commerce, as a salute to the hometown boy who had made good in the corporate world. On the night of the dinner, I went to the airport to pick up David Yunich and escort him to the celebration. I was the assistant business manager for the paper. My predecessor, Gene Robb, the publisher, was chairman of the event.

David Yunich

When I met David at the airport, he asked me if I would drive him to his old neighborhood first. It was a neighborhood of small two-story houses, including the one in which he had been raised. He got out of the car and walked the block in his tuxedo, pausing to look up at a window or to contemplate some past memory. At first, this elegant man in his black tux, strolling the short block, seemed as out of place as Gulliver.

He came back to the car and as we drove to the reception he said, "I know why I'm being honored. It's because they want a Macy's in Albany. I have no problem with that. If it makes sense, we'll have a Macy's here." Then he was silent for a time.

As intimidated as I was by this giant of a man, this chairman of Macy's, I also was able to relax, because he had shown a distinctly human side by walking around his old neighborhood.

"Mr. Yunich," I said, "I feel as though I've known you for such a long time. When I was the office boy at the circulation department, you were a legend. No one had ever sold as many summer subscriptions as you had. And, here I am now in the car with you, the head of Macy's. I've often wondered what the key was."

"It's always the same," he said. "The key to success, in my opinion, is attitude, desire, application and keeping one's self energized. I applied the same energy and enthusiasm in selling subscriptions to the *Times Union* as I did in handling whatever corporate responsibilities were assigned to me. Even though I had gone on to Harvard for my M.B.A., I didn't feel the world owed me anything I did not earn. When I got to Macy's, unlike many of the sophisticates in the organization who relied on a formulaic approach to business, I never ever lost the energy and enthusiasm that I developed selling subscriptions to the *Albany Times Union*."

As a result of his meteoric rise in Macy's, he was elected a director and consultant of several large corporations. At the same time, he was elected President of the New York Chamber of Commerce, the "voice of business" in New York City. He was also involved in many civic activities ranging from being a founding Trustee of Channel 13, New York's Educational Channel, to serving as president of the Greater New York Council of the Boy Scouts.

We later became friends. When I was named publisher of the Albany newspaper, he used to call me his "boy-genius." Actually, he still does, though I have to remind him that "boy" no longer applies. He told me he knew I would be a success from the first time he met me.

Years later, David brought his same energy and enthusiasm to saving New York City's Carnegie Hall when the organization turned to him and asked if he would take on the effort to rescue the world famous concert hall. He agreed to do it. Although there's no plaque to commemorate his work, I never walk by Carnegie Hall without thinking that David Yunich brought the same energy and enthusiasm to saving that great institution that he brought to Macy's, and that he displayed in selling summer subscriptions to the *Albany Times Union*. His commitment was constant.

I remember well when David told me he was "hanging up his spikes" at Macy's. He went on to a series of major league assignments, including serving as chairman of the Metropolitan Transportation Authority. He also served on the boards of Prudential Insurance Co. of America, Fidelity Investments, Nynex, Manufacturers Hanover Bank, W.R. Grace, Carnegie Hall and three universities. He brought them the same nurtured enthusiasm that made him a legend selling summer subscriptions at the Albany newspaper.

❏ ❏ ❏

❝ *I think I sum up my beliefs about leadership in my 'Who's Who' biography where I state: "I admire those men who, whatever their motives, whatever their goals, are inspired to uncommon levels of accomplishment.* **❞**

—David Yunich

❑   ❑   ❑

PART TEN

The Compleat Leader

☐ Master The Nine Powers

☐ Has Staying Power

☐ A Laser Focus

C *ompleat: having all its parts or elements; entire, full, total. Fully accomplished, consummate. Having the maximum extent or degree, thorough* (The New Shorter Oxford English Dictionary).

FRANK A. BENNACK, JR.

Frank Bennack is my idea of the *compleat* leader. He has all of the leadership powers in first-rate form. As a young teenager in San Antonio, Texas, he won a Hearst oratorical contest. The publisher of the newspaper told him that if he ever needed a job that he should come to see him. Frank went off to seminary to become a Catholic priest, but plans changed when he met a young woman in San Antonio and fell in love. He and Luella have been married ever since.

Frank remembered the invitation from the publisher and became a classified advertising salesman, and ultimately, moving through the ranks, became the youngest Hearst publisher at that time. He went on to New York headquarters to run our newspaper company for a few years before becoming President and Chief Executive Officer of the entire corporation. In that position, since 1979, his *compleat* vision of its leadership has permeated the heart of the company in terms of growth, diversity and balance.

When *Business Week* published a cover story about the new leadership at Hearst, and asked Frank about his vision for the corporation, he responded, "Hearst, by the nature of its founder, is the best-known name in publishing. My goal is to make it the best-regarded."

During his tenure as the CEO of Hearst, the company experienced dramatic growth that fulfills his strategic vision. Where others might have seen a blank canvas, he saw a landscape of potential. With a willingness to reach out to projects with a sensible amount of risk, he struck a balance between electronic and print, between newspapers and magazines, between cable channels and traditional television.

Frank Bennack

In 1979, the magazine sector of The Hearst Corporation was the largest monthly magazine company in the world. It still is, but now it boasts of several new magazine starts and acquisitions which have been added to the portfolio.

The broadcast sector of Hearst has grown to become a top-tier premier broadcasting company with television acquisitions in Boston, Kansas City and Dayton, Ohio. The cable and entertainment group of the company was non-existent a decade-and-a-half back, except for the presence of King Features, the world's largest comic and text syndicator. The other assets of the entertainment group developed or acquired during Frank's stewardship include a movie production and distribution company, the cable networks of Lifetime, Arts & Entertainment, ESPN, ESPN2, the History Channel and New England Cable News. All are new to the company. Similarly, the book and business publishing group has continued to be a significant presence.

The newspaper company has been totally restructured. The Hearst Newspapers included those in San Antonio and in Albany (our smallest newspaper), in 1977. The rest were large city, competitive, heavily unionized and, frankly, from a competitive standpoint, disadvantaged newspapers. It took several years to restructure the newspaper company. Gone were those properties which were not destined to become winners, and added were a series of newspapers around the country. The most important and prestigious of these was the acquisition of the Houston Chronicle in 1987. Today, the Hearst newspapers comprise one of the ten largest newspaper groups in the nation, all successful and positioned strongly for the future. All of these accomplishments occurred under the *compleat* leadership of Frank Bennack.

In addition to his full yeast of **Quality, Innovation, Inspiration, Perseverance, Passion, Character, Charisma, Energy** and **Enthusiasm**, Frank has a unique ability to stay with an issue and be intensely focused. When you discuss an issue with Frank, he gives you his complete attention so that it seems that what you have to say is the only thing on his mind. This sense of eye and "thought contact" is constant as is his intensity of pursuit; to be really riveted to the subject, and stay the course until the issue is brought to a conclusion. It has all been a part of the mind-set that he has successfully infused into the whole organization.

Frank likes to talk about how the mind-set of a leader creates and cultivates the strategies that invite others to join in the achievement of that mind-set. It's his mind-set that causes our collective performance to be so outstanding, as gauged by the public companies we monitor and compare ourselves with. It is a mind-set that works in good times, as well as in times we wish were better.

We've faced some very difficult challenges during the almost twenty years I've been the head of the newspaper company with Hearst. Frank is always supportive and at your shoulder when you're facing the worst of circumstances.

We faced an unusual situation because the paper he ran early in his career, the *San Antonio Light*, was historically the afternoon newspaper. That was the newspaper he had grown up with. It competed with Rupert Murdoch's morning *San Antonio Express News*. Even though we became a morning newspaper, we were never the natural morning paper. The *Express News* had the better demographics and the better advertising profile. This didn't matter much when the market was robust, but when the Texas depression hit in 1984, and both newspapers were severely affected, we were hurt more at the *Light*.

We brought in an outstanding publisher, George Irish, and fought the battle for several years. However, it became increasingly obvious that if we wished to remain in San Antonio, we had to join the rest of America and become a one newspaper city; the advertising base was simply not strong enough to support two competing newspapers.

There was only one thing left to do. We developed a strategic objective to acquire the *Express News*, which we did. We had to satisfy the U.S. Department of Justice requirements to seek new owners for the *Light*. Unfortunately, there were no buyers, so we had to close our own newspaper in order to acquire the competitive *Express News*. And I must say, we did that in a highly professional way by placing all of the employees through the most massive job placement program that the professional firm we engaged had ever seen. I can't think of anything else we've had to do in restructuring the newspaper company that has had the same trauma and drama as this.

When we went to San Antonio to tell our employees that we were closing our own newspaper to buy the competition, Frank Bennack was right there. "This was my newspaper and my hometown; I will face the music on this one," he said to me. This was a difficult and emotional event. Without flinching, he stood up before our colleagues and not only spoke to them, but addressed their fears and concerns.

This is a typical response for Frank Bennack. Whenever there has been a difficult situation that had to be confronted, Frank has been there. He's a striving man, and he instills in his colleagues a desire to strive too. No matter how well we have done in our individual media sector groups, he is always raising the bar higher, his mind-set seeking the next level of success. If those of us who lead institutional operations do not share our mind set, then that vision never really stands a chance of being fulfilled.

This is not some management tool that he has devised, but a way to do what is possible rather than settle for what is easily deliverable. He has caused those of us who are his associates to think the same way. That's a constant characteristic. He is also very innovative. There are so many examples of magazines that we have launched, new businesses that we have created, whole new institutional capabilities such as new media activities, that started with Frank's imagination and his willingness to cultivate new concepts.

◻ ◻ ◻

I n short, Frank Bennack has been an extraordinary leader, competent in all the various sectors of the media industry. He has a great and intimate knowledge of every single one of more than one hundred Hearst businesses, and a great passion for the pursuit of excellence everywhere.

All this, too, with a sense of humor.

The Hearst Corporation, almost invisible before Frank assumed the presidency and the position of CEO, embarked on a series of communication efforts for our own employees as well as those who might become part of the corporation through acquisition. A unique publication, a beautiful silver colored booklet, summarized the background of the company and focused on each of the individual sectors, including a photo page of the leadership group in each one of our business sectors. The newspaper group picture included the senior corporate managers and each of the editors from our major papers around the country. This showed the readers the outstanding editorial talents we had nationwide. It was our way of communicating our commitment to a quality editorial product.

The editors were brought to New York and were photographed as an assembled group. Inadvertently, a year passed between that photo session and publication of the book. In that time, it was natural that some of those editors moved on to other positions and had been replaced. The ad agency told us their absence was not a problem. They would simply pose the new editors in similar positions and strip their photos into the originals — so far, so good. However, unbeknownst to us, when the new photos didn't quite fit, the ad agency stripped only the heads and repasted them onto the bodies of the previous editors. The brochure got printed that way. After all, it didn't need to be proofread; these were simple routine photos.

It was published with the wrong heads on the wrong bodies.

Time Magazine was tipped off and ran a press section shot of the photo. In fact, *Time* showed the heads identifying whom the bodies originally belonged to. Our public salute was becoming a true embarrassment. The day the *Time Magazine* piece hit the stands, Frank Bennack called a few of us into his office, including fellow project coordinator Ben Srere, and said, "My God, have you seen what's happened?" The three of us then sat silently with *Time Magazine* splayed in front of us, a winner-take-all expression on its glossy face.

The silver cover booklet was the first and most public communication effort under Frank's administration; we were speechless. It was bad enough that heads were pasted on the wrong bodies, but now it seemed that some heads were going to roll. I thought, "this is the worst thing that could have happened." Suddenly, Frank looked up and said, "you know, there's only one thing for us to do in a situation like this." He paused for a moment and then burst out laughing. Of course, Ben and I joined right in.

This situation was typical of Frank's leadership; the right touch of levity kept a serious situation from becoming overwhelming.

And so, as I reflect on all the various people I have known who have crossed my path, I have selected one person who has always turned up the flame of those individual traits of "the leader within you." Frank Bennack is the most singular example of testimony to all those powers and he is never without them. They are constantly available and are fueled from within. It's a true inspiration to be associated with him and always a challenge to measure up to the way he chooses to approach his life. The threads of his life are woven inextricably and brilliantly into the tapestry that is the Hearst corporation.

REFLECTIONS ON

F R A N K A. B E N N A C K, J R.

By: Shelley Ann Bennack McCullough,
Frank A. Bennack, Jr.'s Daughter

*W*hile growing up, my four younger sisters and I were most aware of those characteristics of my father that directly, and sometimes adversely, impacted on us. For me, his intensity of focus translated into the old adage, "if it's worth doing, it's worth doing right!" This perfectionism sometimes seemed more a burden than a blessing when I looked to my father for help. I can recall more than a few late night sessions working on school projects that I would have preferred to knock-out quickly, whatever the cost in quality. However, if Dad was going to help, he was going to teach you that good work takes commitment, patience and perseverance.*

The other trait of my father, that I remember learning about the hard way was his emphasis on character. Unfortunately, or so I thought at the time, my mother was equally devoted to honesty, integrity and responsibility. When my girlfriends' parents wrote them "doctor appointment notes" so they could leave school early to get their hair done before a big dance, my parents steadfastly refused to lie. On one occasion, my parents took us out of school for a special family excursion. Instead of writing a note claiming illness, my parents wrote a note explaining that we had gone to a lodge at Eagle Lake, the honesty of which failed to impress the school authorities and was rewarded with an unexcused absence on our records!

Over time, my sisters and I have grown to appreciate the value of these early lessons and my father's qualities. As an attorney, I have, from time to time, found myself mightily inconvenienced by my own stubborn sense of integrity. Inconveniences, yet still proud of the values my father helped instill in me.

Now adults, with careers and families of our own, the lawyer, doctor and artists, that as small girls sometimes chafed at my father's intensity of focus, today gratefully count on it, and him, in difficult times. When we have problems, we turn to my mother for comfort and my father for solutions. My father's philosophy of there being no problem that can't be solved if we apply innovation, inspiration, perseverance, passion, charisma, energy and enthusiasm (and if we stay true to the basics of good character) helps guide our path. We know that no matter how many other demands there are on my father's time, we will ultimately get 110% of his attention for our dilemmas and that invariably, he'll help us find a way to accomplish the impossible.

PART ELEVEN

Your Tapestry

- ❐ Who Has Helped With Your Tapestry?
- ❐ Who Has Mastered The Nine Powers?
- ❐ Continue The Quest For Excellence

wenty-five years ago, I read a column by a man named Father John Reidy, who set out a way for us to describe who we really are. As an exercise, he suggested taking paper and pen and writing down the names of six people who, throughout the course of your life, have influenced you. Next, you were to name the quality about them that you remembered most.

When you add up those six qualities, they are probably a fair representation of who you are as an individual. Sometimes there may only be a few such people, but there is always some characteristic that found a way to infuse itself within you and caused you to nourish that power as you grew throughout the years.

We all want to be motivated to reach for a higher standard. People want to know that there are common powers that they can replicate and take into their own lives. They can borrow from them. These people comprise your threads of life.

These threads of life that appear before you may only appear as a momentary whisp, but if you can see them, if your eye can catch the vision and you can take hold of them, then, one-by-one, they begin to weave the tapestry of your life. You need only be open to discovering them and you have to be willing to embrace them.

I began this book with images of threads, the threads of life, that go into making the tapestry of life. I want to conclude this way. I would not be in the position that I'm in today, if I hadn't been open to receiving the leadership gifts that became a part of my natural fabric.

Today, the Hearst organization has some 13,000 individuals contributing their creativity, energy and competency. I want to single out the group that has constantly nourished me with its unlimited leadership.

Chief among those threads is the keen intellect and artistry of interests of Chief Operating Officer Gil Maurer; the calm, penetrating mind and orderly demeanor of Executive Vice President and Book Group Head Vic Ganzi; the energy, candor and drive of Television Group Head John Conomikes; the gentlemanly refinement and wide-gauge scope of Cable and Entertainment Group Head Ray Joslin; the vibrant enthusiasm and crisp precision of Magazine Group Head Cathie Black; the steady perseverance and personal striving of Controller Tom Hughes; the clear thinking and robust instinctive leadership of Newspaper Group Executive George Irish; the easy manner and rich capability range of Newspaper Group Executive Lee Guittar; and comforting insight of General Counsel Jon Thackary.

The tapestry is still being sewn . . .

A Final Interlude
Apply The Nine Powers To Your Own Life

Your personal tapestry is a vivid and beautiful picture of all those individual threads that have come your way. Each thread represents a person. Some threads are of the strongest sinew that weave the mosaic tapestry of the leader within you.

Pause and reflect on the six people who have had the most profound impact on your leadership tapestry. List them here. After each name write just a simple sentence which best describes the characteristic in them that most powerfully influenced you.

When your list is complete, take a few minutes to examine quietly the individual threads you have chosen. These threads weave together and are a brilliant reflection of your tapestry.

MY PERSONAL THREADS OF LIFE

- ☐ _____
- ☐ _____
- ☐ _____
- ☐ _____
- ☐ _____
- ☐ _____
- ☐ _____
- ☐ _____

SEEKING YOUR PATHMAKERS & KINDLERS

Your life and career have been indelibly influenced by people who have crossed your path and shared their strongest leadership powers with you. Each of them has been a lighthouse helping you define your course.

Acknowledge them here. For each of the nine powers of leadership which have been presented to you in *The Leader Within You* — identify the person who has crossed your path and kindled your own leadership.

Quality _____

Innovation _____

Inspiration _____

Perseverance _____

Passion _____

Character _____

Charisma _____

Energy _____

Enthusiasm _____

More Endorsements For *The Leader Within You*

"Bob Danzig is a leader. He is uniquely qualified to share his years of experience and leadership skills in this superb book."
—**Wesley Turner, Publisher,**
Fort Worth Star Telegram

"Bob Danzig effectively addresses the qualities of leadership in ways that can be understood and used . . . is a must read."
—**Larry Franklin, President/CEO**
Harte-Hanks Communications, Inc.

"Bob Danzig has been a leader in his field and in his company for a long time. Now, happily, the rest of us can benefit from the wisdom of the man himself."
— **William R. Burleigh, President & CEO,**
E.W. Scripps Company

"Bob has found the leader in himself and, in this book, tells how you can develop your own individual powers of leadership."
—**Anthony Mazzola**
Former Editor-in-Chief, *Harper's Bazaar*

"*The Leader Within You* is a must read for all who aspire to leadership roles. Absolutely smashing."
—**Bernard F. Connors, Chairman**
British American Publishing

"Bob Danzig personifies those qualities that are identifiable in great leaders. His sense of fair play, hard work, inquisitive mind, creativity, character, and enthusiasm have brought him to the top of his company and his industry. All of us who have known Bob well have been rewarded by his passion and his compassion, two qualities that every leader needs."

—Malcom A. Borg,
Chairman of the Board, *The Bergen Record*

"Bob Danzig believes the quality of leadership is within every person, and to a great degree, I agree. His book, however, may be most useful for those who are curious, skeptical or hopeful. The format will make it easier for the reader to make his own decision."

—Stanford Lipsey,
President, *Buffalo Evening News*

"If anyone in this country is qualified to write about leadership, it's certainly Bob Danzig."

—Joe Oldham, Editor, *Popular Mechanics*

"Bob Danzig was born with the leader within him. You can find out if you have the same quality when you read the book."

—Carl E. Touhey, President of Touhey Associates

"Bob Danzig is a leader and an inspiration for thousands of newspapermen and women. His ideas about how to nurture the qualities of leadership will empower anyone wanting to develop personal leader skills. There's no better time for a book on personal leadership qualities and no better person to write it than Bob Danzig. He has set the pace, provided the inspiration, shown the perseverance and character and sparked the inspiration for so many of us in newspapers. The punch and power of his ideas make this a must-read."

—John F. Oppedahl,
Publisher & CEO, *The Arizona Republic*

"Bob Danzig speaks from years of experience and success when he writes about leadership qualities."

—Malcolm W. Applegate,
President, Indianapolis Newspapers, Inc.

"The story of Hearst is very inspiring and Bob Danzig's leadership is instrumental in the company's great growth and success. That's why *The Leader Within You* is so important to read."
— **John W. Madigan,**
Chairman, Tribune Company

"Bob Danzig practiced leadership and now explains it in a book rich with insight and experience."
— **James F. Hoge, Jr., Editor,** *Foreign Affairs*

"Bob Danzig's irrepressible spirit has inspired many a newspaper man and woman. Now he shares the key leadership traits learned from 46 years of newspapering. That's quite a gift to those of us still plowing fields Bob long ago harvested."
— **Jay Smith, President, Cox Newspapers, Inc.**

"Bob Danzig should have been an obstetrician! Thousands of new leaders will be born from the lessons learned in *The Leader Within You*."
— **Frank R.J. Whittaker, VP-Operations,**
McClatchy Newspapers

"Bob Danzig has managed and led through a period of enormous change in American society and business. The nine leadership traits and skills that he identifies transcend changes and will help any leader be more effective."
— **Frank Blethen, Publisher,** *Seattle Times*

"Bob Danzig is one of those magic people who, when he enters a room, he fills it. And when he begins to speak, he owns it."
— **Paul La Camera, VP/General Manager,**
WCVB-TV, Boston, Massachusetts

"*The Leader Within You* concentrates on nine basic essentials for success, as identified by the author, Robert Danzig, who has an overabundance of each element."
— **Scott C. Schurz, Vice President,**
Schurz Communications Inc.

"Bob Danzig is one of the most respected figures in the U.S. newspaper industry. He's learned a lot about leadership in one of the toughest businesses there is, and he shares it all."

—Max Jennings
Editor, *Dayton Daily News*

"Most experts on leadership extol the virtues of great men and women to demonstrate the essence of good leadership. Bob Danzig uncovers the leadership traits within each of us and inspires us to use them to the best of our ability. The clarity and persuasiveness of his message are overpowering. Once you've read *The Leader Within You*, you will know how to create a mind set and then nurture your personal qualities to become a successful leader."

—R. Mark Sullivan, President,
The College of Saint Rose, Albany, New York

"If it is possible for a book to make *eye* contact, *The Leader Within You* does it. Bob Danzig empowers the next generation of leaders with his work."

—Jim Hefner,
Vice President & General Manager,
WTAE-TV, Pittsburgh

"Yours is the very best American success story and your message meant a great deal."

—Lillian Kopenhaver, Associate Dean
Florida International University

"Thank you for providing an important thread of inspiration and information for the lives of students and faculty."

—Ernest C. Hynds,
Journalism Department Chair,
University of Georgia

"Thank you again for giving back what you have learned throughout your career. It would be a tremendous help for me to have the benefit of your knowledge and advice."

—Alexander Major, President,
Major Health Services

"Everyone appreciated the bright light you shed . . . and the clarity, eloquence and passion with which you voiced your convictions about leadership."
—Anthony Oettinger,
Program on Information Resources Policy Chair,
Harvard University

"Your passion is evident in your presentation, and the manner in which you personalize your message is compelling."
—John F. Flynn, President, YMCA

"Thank you for speaking at our sales rally. It was clear that you are well acquainted with 'walking the walk,' not just 'talking the talk' when it comes to pursuing the most difficult goals."
—Dwight M. Brown, VP of Advertising,
Houston Chronicle

"Your wonderful anecdotes, skillfull delivery and warm relationship with the audience held them spellbound."
—Mary Lynn Martin,
Associate Director, American Press Institute

"I just wanted to tell you how inspiring I found your talk. Thank you for reminding us of what is most important."
—David Hughey,
***The Herald Sun*, Durham, NC**

"To suggest that your presentation was remarkable is an understatement and does not truly reflect its impact on both my students and myself."
—John H. Shannon,
Dean, Seton Hall University

"Once again, thanks for visiting us. I hope you will return again next year. Good luck with your leadership book."
—Paul Steinle,
University of Miami

"I cannot remember the last time that I was so deeply moved by a speaker. You provided a living confirmation of what we are teaching."

**—Tom Milton, Business Administration
Chairperson, Mercy College**

"It was both a pleasure and privilege to hear your inspirational talk. You certainly make a terrific impression."

**—Jon Knott,
*Albany Times Union***

"I have no hesitancy in declaring — to anyone within earshot — that it was the best speech I have ever heard. Thank You!"

**—Daniel Button, President's Office,
Commission on Independent Colleges & Universities**

"Your speech to the conference was a big hit, engaging us, entertaining us and moving us. I would have liked to hear more of your personal profiles, because each was so poignant and relevant to us all."

**—Richard Chandler,
CEO, Sunrise Medical**

"I think everyone who was present at your wonderful talk . . . found it wise as well as inspiring. We are grateful that you chose to share some of that wisdom with us."

**—Lewis Burke Frankes,
The Writing Center Director,
Marymount Manhattan College**

INDEX